D0517091

Picture Your World in Appliqué

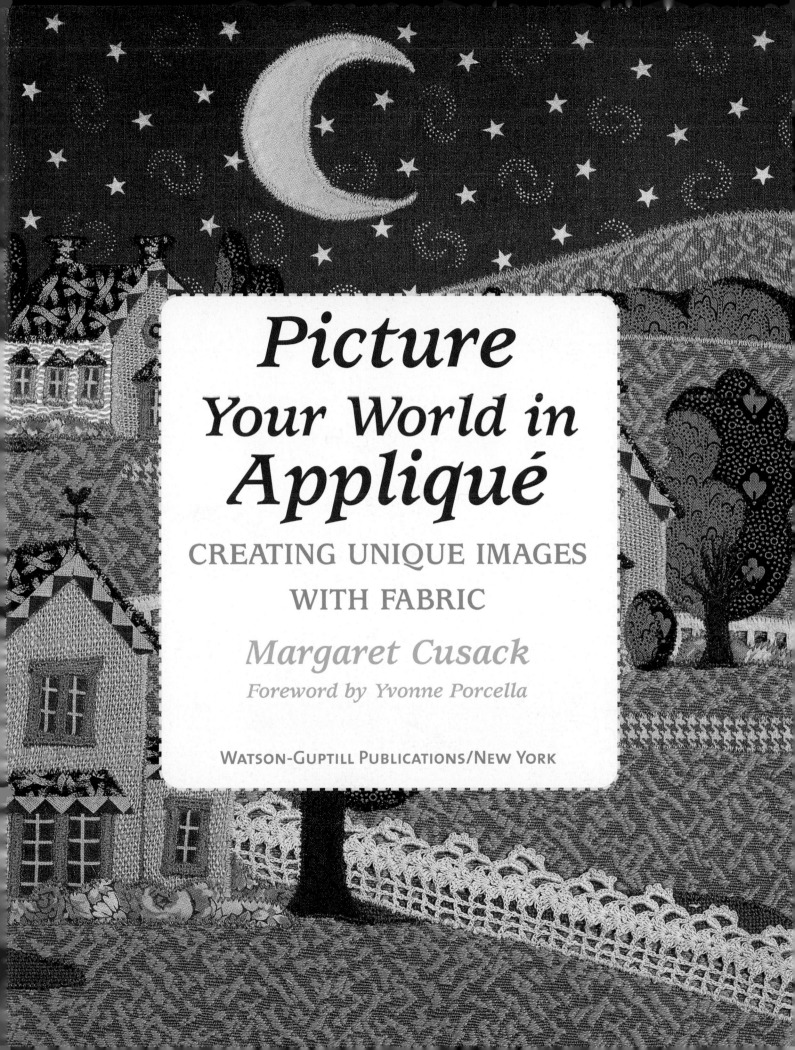

Picture
Your World in
Appliqué

CREATING UNIQUE IMAGES
WITH FABRIC

Margaret Cusack
Foreword by Yvonne Porcella

WATSON-GUPTILL PUBLICATIONS/NEW YORK

For Frank and Kate

Library of Congress Cataloging-in-Publication Data
Cusack, Margaret.
Picture your world in appliqué : creating unique images with
fabric / Margaret Cusack; foreword by Yvonne Porcella.
    p. cm.
Includes bibliographical references and index.
ISBN 0-8230-1641-2
1. Appliqué—Patterns. I. Title.
  TT779.C88 2005
  746.44'5041—dc22
                                            2005009349

All rights reserved. No part of this publication may be
reproduced or used in any form or by any means—graphic,
electronic, or mechanical, including photocopying, recording, taping, or information storage and retrieval systems—
without written permission of the publisher.

Manufactured in the United States of America

First printing, 2005

1 2 3 4 5 6 7 8 9 / 13 12 11 10 09 08 07 06 05

Senior Acquisitions Editor: Joy Aquilino

Project Editor: Andrea Curley

Designer: Sivan Earnest

Production Manager: Hector Campbell

Copyright © 2005 by Margaret Cusack

First published in 2005 by Watson-Guptill Publications,
a division of VNU Business Media, Inc.,
770 Broadway, New York, N.Y. 10003

www.wgpub.com

CREDITS

©Copyright 2005 by Marianne Barcellona, All Rights Reserved for the photographs noted on the following pages: 12 (all), 14 (all), 17 (bottom left), 18 (all), 19 (all), 20 (bottom left), 21, 22, 23, 24, 28 (all), 30 (all), 31 (all), 42 (all), 43 (all), 44 (all), 45 (top right), 46 (all), 47 (all), 48 (all), 49 (all), 51 (all), 52 (first row: top left, top center, top right; second row: bottom left, bottom right), 53 (first row: top left, top right; second row: center left; third row: center left; fourth row: bottom left), 54 (first row: top left, top right; second row: center left, center right; third row: bottom left), 55 (first row: top left, top right; second row: center left; third row: bottom left, bottom center), 59 (all), 60 (all), 61 (all), 62 (all), 63 (all), 66 (all), 68 (all), 69 (all), 70 (all), 71 (all), 72 (all), 73 (all), 78 (all), 79 (all), 80 (all), 81 (all), 87 (all), 88 (all), 89 (all), 90 (all), 91 (all), 96 (all), 97 (all), 98 (all), 100 (top right, center right), 101 (bottom right), 106 (all), 110 (all).

page 1, "Bridal Bouquet" (Detail), 16" x 15" (1985). Commissioned by Avon Products, Inc. for 1986 Centennial Avon calendar.

pages 2–3, "Nighttime," 14" x 20" (1989). Commissioned for and Collection of Kwikset Corporation.

page 36, "City and Country Landscape": Illustration from TROPHIES: Reading Program, Grade 2-1, copyright © 1997 by Harcourt, Inc., reproduced by permission of the publisher.

page 83, "Uncle Ben's Still Life": ®/TM UNCLE BEN'S is a registered trademark of Mars, Incorporated and its affiliates. It is used with permission. Mars, Incorporated is not associated with Margaret Cusack or Watson-Guptill Publications.

page 92, "Harcourt Checkerboard Quilt": Illustrations from "Harcourt Checkerboard Quilt" illustrated by Margaret Cusack, in CHILDREN'S BOOKS 1982–1983: A Graded List of Preschool Through High School, copyright © 1981 by Harcourt, Inc., reprinted by permission of the publisher.

page 102, "My Family Quilt": Illustrations from "My Family Quilt" by Judy Nayer, illustrated by Margaret Cusack, in TROPHIES: Below Level Independent Readers Collection, copyright © 2001 Harcourt, Inc., reprinted by permission of the publisher.

page 120, Alphabet Typefaces: *Extra-Bold Alphabets*, selected and arranged by Dan X. Solo. Mineola, NY: Dover Publications, Inc., 1993.

ACKNOWLEDGMENTS

Thanks to Frank, who has been a wonderful husband and partner, all the while proclaiming my latest artwork his "*new* personal favorite." To our daughter, Kate, for your love and also for keeping me on my toes. To my parents and to Frank's parents for their love and guidance. To friends and relatives who gave me encouragement (and sometimes even shopping bags of fabric!). To my siblings, for their love and support: to my sister Pat Pilchard, who inspired me to become an artist; to my sister Joann Furtner, for mentoring me as a child; to my sister Barbara Jacobson, for her enthusiasm and positive energy; to my brother, James Weaver, for challenging me to be more assertive; and to my sister Deborah Weaver, for her love and friendship and for keeping me sane through all the paperwork of *Picture Your World in Appliqué*.

Thanks to those who contributed their words and knowledge to the book: Tad Crawford of Allworth Publishing; Rick Gottas of The American Art Company; Yvonne Porcella, artist, author, and founder of Studio Art Quilt Associates; Monona Rossol of Arts, Crafts & Theater Safety, Inc. Thanks both to Cheryl McLean, publisher of *Artist to Artist* (Jackson Creek Press), and to William C. MacKay and Rick Campbell, who created *Envisioning Art* (Barnes and Noble, Inc.), for giving me the inspirational quotes I've scattered throughout *Picture Your World in Appliqué*.

Thanks to Paula Nadelstern, Barbara Lee Smith, Michael Fleishman, Jeri Riggs, Deidre Scherer, and other artists who acted as both advisors and cheering squad as I wrote this book.

Thanks to Pratt Institute and to my teachers, especially Martha Mayer Erlebacher. To the Art Institute of Chicago, for the classes I attended there on scholarship as a child. To Barbara Gordon, for introducing me to the world of illustration as my agent for six years. To the ispot and American Showcase for connecting me with illustration clients. To Elly Sienkiewicz, who taught me about fusible webbing. To all the photographers who have taken great care in capturing my stitched artwork on film: Paul Armbruster, Karen Bell, Ron Breland, Alex Cao, Skip Caplan, D. James Dee, Gamma One Conversions, Michel Legrou, and John Milisenda.

Special thanks to Marianne Barcellona, who did a terrific job shooting all of the step-by-step photographs throughout the book.

Thanks to all the art directors, collectors, and clients I've worked with over the last thirty-three years. To Robbie Capp, who introduced me to Watson-Guptill. To my editors, Joy Aquilino and Andrea Curley, to designer Sivan Earnest, and to production manager Hector Campbell, who all worked so hard to make this book become a reality. To my exercise friends, who for twenty-three years have faithfully shown up to share stories and insights as we do our Jane Fonda aerobics tape (". . . drop your knees down to your shoulders, next to your ears").

Thanks to the Society of Illustrators Club, for the fall 2005 retrospective of my work at their beautiful gallery space, and to Director Terry Brown, for his generous sharing of information and advice. To the members of the Textile Study Group of New York, the Graphic Artists Guild, the Society of Children's Book Writers and Illustrators, and the Art Quilt Network/New York, for providing support and high energy.

Thank you all.

"The words 'work' and 'art' are synonyms."
ANONYMOUS

"Pretend you are dancing or singing a picture. A worker or painter should enjoy his work, else the observer will not enjoy it."
PABLO PICASSO

April Showers (Detail)
16" x 15" (1985)
Commissioned by Avon Products, Inc. for 1986 Centennial Avon Calendar

Contents

Foreword

Despite her training as a graphic designer, Margaret Cusack fortunately did not fall prey to the seduction of mere paper and ink. Though her artistic skills are evident in the precise manner in which she creates her realistic illustrations, she chooses to use the medium she has loved since childhood: fabric.

For many years, curious viewers have marveled at the literal nature of Cusack's stitched artwork, which has appeared on magazine covers, packaging, and postage stamps, and in advertisements, calendars, and books. We have all been seduced by her skillful illusions, where netting and lace are transformed into trees and foliage, a chambray shirt pocket holds the sights and sounds of New York City, and quilted farms and houses dot calico landscapes, invariably leaving us to wonder, "Who made this?"

In *Picture Your World in Appliqué* we can all experience Margaret Cusack's world. She discusses her day-to-day artistic life, resourceful storage systems, and unique methods of working, making realism in fabric accessible to everyone. Cusack details how she takes a concept through the process of research, creation, and completion, and offers readers concise instructions, step-by-step photographs, and clear diagrams. The projects, which illustrate themes of family, home, memory, and celebration, along with methods on how to design your own stitched artwork, make this book a must-have for everyone who shares Cusack's love of fabric.

Though she has more than one hundred boxes of fabric in her studio, it is a testament to Cusack's organizational skills that she knows where each color and print is stored, which of her fabrics are vintage, and what she needs to buy new for each project. In the gallery sections throughout the book, her work

is displayed by subject, so that readers can compare her use of value to establish depth in her landscape art, which contrasts sharply with the fabulous dots and checks used in "Self-Portrait in Checkerboard" (see page 55). She also shows how to use small-scale prints and textured fabrics to convey a variety of moods, as in her colorful "Holiday Tree" project (see page 105).

Cusack is also renowned for always having information on the current marketplace, design trends, and professional contacts at her fingertips. In this day of computers and electronic notebooks, it's ironic and gives us all courage to learn that an old-fashioned Rolodex is one of the keys to her successful career, which has spanned more than thirty years. She shares some of these invaluable connections in *Picture Your World in Appliqué* by including advice from notable industry professionals: health and safety guidelines from an industrial hygienist, copyright information from an attorney, and framing options for stitched artwork from a professional framer. As an added bonus, for inspiration she includes quotes by famous artists.

Sharing her talents, techniques, and professional approach to the marketplace are the hallmarks of Margaret Cusack's personality. I applaud her achievements in *Picture Your World in Appliqué*.

&. Yvonne Porcella

An artist specializing in wearable art and art quilts, Yvonne Porcella began in 1962 by making unique garments and woven wall hangings and in 1980 exhibited her first art quilt. Her work has toured internationally and is actively collected by individuals, corporations, and museums. Author of nine books on clothing patterns, fabric painting, and quilt patterns, Yvonne Porcella is founder of Studio Art Quilt Associates.

Hands
144" x 108" (1992)
Margaret Cusack, "Hands,"
Stitched Art Installation.
Collection of The Culinary
Institute of America.

Introduction

Fabric. The smooth texture of a lavender silk, the rich color of a blue velvet, the raucous chartreuse/tangerine prints of the 1960s. A soft baby blanket, the crisp serge of a three-button business suit, or a summer breeze on a cotton skirt—to me, it's all about the fabric. I have always loved it, and it's always had a profound effect on me.

As a child, my reaction to fabric was truly visceral. I hated the scratchy wool scarves that my mother wanted me to wear. I loved the sophisticated coolness of the satiny Halloween costumes that my older sisters made for me. I cried when I outgrew my starched white blouse with the stitched Jack and Jill climbing up one side of my collar and down the other. I can close my eyes and still remember the tweed fabric of my father's jacket and the warm sunlight on my mother's summer dress.

I have always loved fabric, but unfortunately sewing has never been my forte. Making use of fabric in traditional ways, with all those buttonholes and zippers, has never really interested me. However, since high school, even though I didn't sew, I always kept a box of fabric at hand—not for making clothes, but just because I liked the colors and textures.

Most people see fabric as something to use for making drapes or slipcovers or clothing. But over time I became more and more interested in using fabric to make art. Where other people see horizontal stripes, I see stairs. Where others see velvets, I see clouds. I take fabric's ready-made texture, pattern, and color—the polka dots, the tweeds, and the prints—and use them in my own way. To me fabric is memory, nostalgia, and emotion; and I use it to convey those feelings in my work.

As a result, I have turned my love of fabric into a career.

To describe myself: I am an artist. I create "Norman Rockwell" realism out of stitchery and fabric. Most of my work is used as illustrations in magazines, books, posters, and ads. I also do portraits and large-scale hangings for private and corporate commissions—all in fabric. Some of my work involves hand embroidery, but most of it is machine-appliqué, (appliqué is somewhat like a jigsaw puzzle made out of pieces of fabric and sewn down with zigzag stitching).

As an artist-illustrator, I balance the needs of my clients while meeting some near-impossible deadlines—two weeks, a few days, or even overnight. I incorporate my own sense of design, color, and composition within the restrictions of the project at hand.

I was trained as a graphic designer and have always loved drawing and typography. Many artists have influenced my work: Toulouse-Lautrec, Manet, Picasso,

This photograph shows me on my mother's lap. I was about four years old.

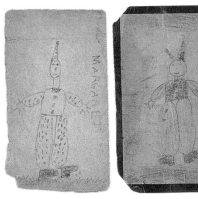

Even at that young age, I loved to draw.

Silent Night
16¹/4" x 13¹/4" (1983)
Commissioned by Harcourt, Brace, Jovanovich, Inc. for *The Christmas Carol Sampler*

"Every child is an artist. The problem is how to remain an artist once he grows up."
PABLO PICASSO

Ben Shahn, Grandma Moses, Norman Rockwell, Klimt, Cezanne, and others. For this reason, I've included quotes from artists and other creative people throughout *Picture Your World in Appliqué*. I hope you enjoy their words and benefit from their insights.

Over the years, at exhibitions and slide presentations of my stitched artwork, people have asked: "How did you get started?" "How long does it take to do your artwork?" "Is there a book on your work?"

"Is there a book on your work?" *That's* the question that prompted me to write *Picture Your World in Appliqué.* The person who asked it was a young French quilter whose group was visiting my studio. Her interest in a book made me realize that the time was right for me finally to put my stitched art career into words. Though some of my work has appeared in books and magazines, until now there hasn't been one book featuring my entire career. I'm thankful to Watson-Guptill Publications for the opportunity to present my work to you now.

Picture Your World in Appliqué will show you my technique of creative machine-stitched appliquéd artwork. Though many of my images look complex, my process is actually rather simple. I hope you will adapt it into your own techniques and that the projects included here will help you develop your own designs. This book is also intended for those who do not sew but who are intrigued by stitched artwork. With those readers in mind, and also to give inspiration to those who *do* want to take on the projects in *Picture Your World in Appliqué*, I've added a gallery of images after each chapter. Included are many stitched illustrations that have been used in magazines, advertisements, and children's books.

The seven projects in *Picture Your World in Appliqué* will be of interest to both the novice and the more experi-

enced fabric artist. Some, such as "Vase of Flowers," the "Holiday Tree" hanging, and the "Welcome Home" banner are simple. Others, such as "Down on the Farm," "Nostalgic Portrait," "Family Tree," and "Floral Border" are more challenging. I hope you will try them all.

Chapter 1, "Setting Up Your Work Space," will show you the tools and materials that I use to create my stitched artwork. Also included are storage tips and methods on how I've organized my studio. I hope that these ideas will help you in organizing your own work space. Also, safety expert Monona Rossol supplies important information about adhesives, ergonomics, lighting, ventilation, and other topics. Following Chapter 1 is a selection of my appliquéd cityscape images.

In Chapter 2 I've used my landscape "Down on the Farm" to explain how to create your own pattern by using reference photos, sketches, copier machines, tracing paper, etc., as well as tips on composition. Lawyer Tad Crawford has contributed "Copyright Ins and Outs," an important discussion about how to protect your own artwork, as well as how to avoid infringing on the copyrights of others. Following Chapter 2 is a gallery featuring my appliquéd landscapes.

Chapter 3, "Creating Your Artwork," takes "Down on the Farm" to completion with step-by-step instructions. I've included exercises on color and information about fusible webbing and light boxes. Rick Gottas, who has been framing artwork for more than thirty years, has contributed "Framing Stitched Artwork," a complete discussion on the subject. Following Chapter 3 I've given you a behind-the-scenes look at how I created some of my stitched artwork. In addition to the finished images, I've included the preliminary sketches, reference photos, and patterns of some of my important artwork.

The instructions for "Floral Border" in Chapter 4 will show you how to create a decorative border, as well as adapt your image to picture frames, pillows, scrapbook covers, and greeting cards. Following this chapter are some of my fused fabric images, as well as some dimensional stitched artwork.

The "Welcome Home" banner and the instructions in Chapter 5 explain how to make a colorful celebration banner that also can be adapted to include the names of your friends and/or family. This chapter is followed by a selection of my appliquéd hangings.

"Vase of Flowers" in Chapter 6 introduces selective padding—adding dimension to specific areas of your stitched artwork. To make "Vase of Flowers," you can purchase new floral fabrics or make use of favorite floral fabrics that you have on hand. Following Chapter 6 is a sampling of my appliquéd still life images.

"Family Tree" in Chapter 7 shows how to create a quilted effect in this personalized genealogical, "soon-to-be"

heirloom. It concludes with a selection of my quilted images.

"Nostalgic Portrait" in Chapter 8 will help you transform your favorite photograph into an appliquéd portrait. To further inspire you, I've included a gallery of some of my appliquéd images of people.

"Holiday Tree" in Chapter 9 will show you how to make an appliquéd holiday tree, great as a festive gift or as a colorful decoration for your own home. It involves adding sequins, charms, beads, and bits of jewelry to this colorful project. This chapter concludes with a selection of my favorite appliquéd holiday images.

After thirty-three years of creating stitched artwork, my one box of fabric has grown to be more than a hundred boxes, each filled to the brim with wonderful fabrics. My response to the French quilter is, yes, now there is a book on my work: *Picture Your World in Appliqué.*

Here are some of the projects in *Picture Your World in Appliqué.*

CHAPTER 1

Setting Up Your Work Space

As writer Virginia Woolf would agree, it's important to have your own work space. In order to create, you have to claim a space in your home (or elsewhere) that you can call your own. It's crucial to be able to work, make a mess, and then close the door on it, knowing that only you will open that door, and that you will show your work to others only when you are ready. The creative process needs space and, sometimes, even isolation.

But, no matter what size your work space is, it's easy to fill it up. For that reason, storage and organization are crucial. The main thing is to be able to find what you need, *when* you need it. It's important to settle on storage methods that are right for you. The storage solutions that I've developed may be a help to you, and I will go into detail on them in this chapter. But before you can store your materials and supplies, you need to know about them, which is what the following sections discuss.

This is a view of my studio. (Most of the time it is not as neat as it is shown here!)

Fabrics

"Creativity is a habit, and the best creativity is the result of good work habits."
TWYLA THARP

People always ask me where I buy my fabric. The answer is simple—everywhere! I buy fabric wherever I go, whether I'm in a department store or at a tag sale. I even buy fabric when I'm on a vacation. Since the size of most of my images is 18" x 24" or smaller, when I shop, I usually buy just a yard of a particular fabric, which will be enough to last quite a long time. I buy intuitively, knowing that I will always make use of textured whites for clouds and unusual greens for landscapes. Certain fabrics "speak" to me and I allow myself to respond to them on an emotional level—buying what I think will add to my palette of colors and textures.

Since many fabrics are sold seasonally, unless I buy a fabric when I see it, that particular fabric may not be available when I need it later. Therefore, I buy what I think will be useful for both current and future projects.

Because of my frugal "waste not, want not" upbringing, I do not cut fabric from clothing if the item is still usable. Therefore, I don't buy clothing with the intention of later cutting it up for my projects.

Since most of my images are rather small, I seek out fabrics in which the pattern is not too large in scale. And, depending on the project, I also consider the fabric's overall texture and whether it is sheer, opaque, or flexible. Normally, I avoid fabrics that are stretchy, but a costume-oriented illustration commission for Sadlier Publishing introduced me to spandex fabric. The fabric's unique stretchiness was very useful in creating the costumes.

In addition to the assorted fabrics you will be using in the *Picture Your World in Appliqué* projects, I've also suggested using:

- white cotton duck fabric and lightweight white batiste fabric for backing
- white felt and batting for padding.

These are useful materials to have on hand for any project that you may take on.

Fabric Shopping for Large Projects

My boxes contain a great variety of fabrics that are useful for projects that are 18" x 24" or smaller. I can usually find just about everything I need in my fabric supplies. However, when I'm working on a large project (some commissions have been 8' to 12' long), I need much larger pieces of fabric than what's on hand. So I choose the palette of colors and fabrics and create a rough fabric paste-up. (A rough fabric paste-up is a smaller and more spontaneous version of the completed project, showing the final selection of fabrics glued or taped in position.

SCALE

The size (or scale) of the print or pattern will have a big impact on your project. For example, when buying fabric for the project in Chapter 6, "Vase of Flowers," if you choose a floral print fabric with very large flowers and then decide on a fabric with a large print for the border, the two may compete too much for the viewer's attention.

When shopping and making decisions about fabrics, make an L-shape out of the thumb and index finger of each hand. Use the two Ls to visually crop your fabrics to the size that you envision for your project. This will give you an idea of whether that particular fabric will suit the shape that you are considering. Then decide if the print is suitable.

You'll be making your own in Chapter 3.) To create the rough fabric paste-up, I make use of the fabrics that I have on hand, even though I am aware that there may not be quite enough of some fabrics to complete the large project. Once the rough fabric paste-up is finalized and approved, I estimate how much of each fabric is needed and then shop to find equivalent fabrics to match my initial choices. Living in New York City has an advantage in that there are many fabric stores available. However, if I lived in an area with fewer fabric stores, I would probably purchase fabric from catalogs.

HINT
When shopping for fabric, if you have a certain color in mind but don't have a swatch in that specific color, you could:
- use paint store color swatches
- paint a piece of paper to match the color you have in mind
- cut swatches of color from magazine photos.

Then, with these swatches in hand, shop for the fabrics that you need.

My collection of flesh-colored fabrics was useful in creating "Joy to the World."

"Joy to the World," 31" x 26 1/4" (1983), was included in a book of songs that features people of many nationalities. Commissioned by Harcourt, Brace, Jovanovich, Inc. for *The Christmas Carol Sampler*

Art Supplies

FOAM CORE

Foam core is white board that is a sandwich made up of two sheets of white cover stock paper that has a layer of soft Styrofoam in the middle. I use foam core for mounting small stitched artwork. It is sold in $\frac{1}{4}$" and $\frac{1}{2}$" thicknesses and is available in several sizes. The 30"-x-40" sheets are a convenient size. Store them horizontally, so that they do not warp.

CANVAS STRETCHERS

I stretch finished stitched artwork on canvas stretchers, so I keep a supply of canvas stretchers in a variety of sizes on hand. The stretchers are available at art stores and come in many sizes in 1" increments. I keep a chart of the sizes to know what I have on hand.

PENS AND PENCILS

Pigma Micron pens are available in a variety of colors and in several sizes. They are great for creating a thin line that will not "bleed," i.e., the inked line "stays put" on the fabric and will not expand as it is absorbed by the fabric.

As a matter of personal taste, I use a #2 or #3 lead pencil when I do my sketches. Pencils with harder lead (#4 or #5) are useful for more detailed sketches because they create a "crisper" line.

Stabilo pencils have a crayonlike quality that is good for drawing on a variety of fabrics. They come in an assortment of colors, plus black and white.

I also use acrylic paints, carbon paper, markers, colored pencils, and/or watercolor when I need to create a full-color version of my sketches.

TRACING MATERIALS

To create the main drawing, I use tracing paper or vellum (a heavier version of tracing paper). As you will see in Chapter 2, the transparency of tracing paper allows you to easily make changes, additions, and erasures to your drawing. When the finished drawing becomes your pattern, the tracing paper's transparency will allow you to trace the pattern's lines onto the fabric.

Acetate is also useful. However, if you are going to use a copier machine to print your drawing onto acetate, make sure to use "transparency film" meant "for plain paper copiers." Transparency film is available in stationery stores and it is usually used to make overhead projection transparencies. Other acetates may melt in some copier machines.

ADHESIVES

In the projects of *Picture Your World in Appliqué*, I use one adhesive (spray adhesive) to temporarily attach the fabric shapes to the backing fabric. I use another adhesive (fusible webbing, which is a thin layer of dry adhesive that is activated by pressing it with a hot iron) to permanently attach the fusible webbing to the back of the fabrics. Once the fusible webbing-backed fabric shapes are cut out, they are sprayed with the spray adhesive, positioned onto the backing fabric, and fused in place by ironing them.

The fusible webbing that I use is paper-backed, so it can be ironed onto the back of fabrics easily. The paper backing is also helpful in tracing shapes for projects. I buy fusible webbing in a large roll from the manufacturer, but it can be purchased by the yard in most fabric stores.

I have tried many spray adhesives and have found 3M Spraymount to be the best for my work. The sprayed mist is fine rather than splotchy, and the glue itself is not too thick, as some other adhesives are. The sprayed fabric can be repositioned without leaving a residue.

Gudy paper is rub-on paper-backed adhesive that is archival.

Both white glue and glue sticks are useful for gluing down small pieces of fabric.

Canvas stretchers are sold in a variety of lengths in 1" increments. I staple my completed artwork onto assembled canvas stretchers.

Colored pencils are a quick way to make color choices in small sketches. See page 69 for my colored pencil sketch of "Welcome Home" Banner.

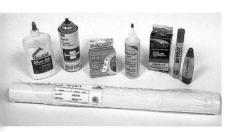

A variety of adhesives are useful for different purposes. From left to right, I use white glue, spray adhesive, glue dots, clear adhesive, roll-on glues, and paper-backed adhesive.

Equipment

SEWING MACHINE

When I began doing stitched artwork, I used a Singer Touch-and-Sew machine for a long time. For the last fifteen years or so, I have used a Bernina 1130 sewing machine. After using it for many years, my Bernina is not exactly up-to-date, but it suits me very well and is like a favorite pen or pencil to me. I occasionally use some of the decorative stitches on my sewing machine, but I mostly use the zigzag stitch and the running stitch.

There are many sewing machines on the market, and you should consider your own needs and research the capabilities of each one. Whatever machine you use, it's important to keep it serviced and in "good health." Cleaning and oiling your sewing machine are critical.

My machine is built into a custom-made L-shaped counter/worktable (that was recycled from a solid wooden door). The counter also includes my light box and additional storage areas.

IRONING EQUIPMENT

I always iron the fabrics that I've chosen for each project. Since I don't have enough space in my studio for a traditional ironing board, I created a rectangular ironing board surface on part of a large drafting table. And when I need to iron larger pieces of fabric, I make a temporary 24"-x-72" ironing board area on my worktable using blankets covered with a sheet.

When needed, I use household spray starch and a sheer cotton pressing cloth.

ARTOGRAPH

I use an Artograph, an enlarging/reducing device that projects my sketches onto my drawing table or onto the floor. Its benefit is that it has a wide range; it can enlarge images up to approximately 60" and reduce them down to 1" or less.

Since this is an expensive tool, you might not want to purchase one. Instead, you can use a copier machine with enlarging and reducing capabilities. You can also have images enlarged or reduced at your local copier store. Or, if you are adept with a computer, you can assemble your image on your computer screen, enlarging and reducing the different parts of your sketches.

> *"Art class was like a religious ceremony to me. I would wash my hands carefully before touching paper or pencils. The instruments of work were sacred objects to me."*
> JOAN MIRÓ

COPIER MACHINE

When I am creating my pattern, I use a copier machine to enlarge and flop images (by printing them on tracing paper and using the reverse side of the printed image). I also do copies of my sketches onto paper, acetate, or tracing paper. Again, since you may not want to invest in such an expensive piece of equipment, you can go to a copy store with your images.

COMPUTER

I have a Macintosh computer that I use to design and print lettering. At this time I do not use the computer as a design tool. However, for those of you who would like to, there are many programs that are helpful in designing patterns and images. At present the most popular ones include PhotoShop, Illustrator, and InDesign.

I've used my Bernina 1130 sewing machine for many years.

I use spray starch and a pressing cloth when I iron my fabrics. The tacking iron is useful in ironing small pieces of fabric.

My Artograph projector is wall-mounted and can project a sketch or photo so I can trace it onto fabric or paper.

HINT

If you are serious about your artwork, it is crucial to document it with professional photography as slides or larger chromes. (Keeping a record of what you've accomplished will help you secure new commissions.) If you are not able to accurately photograph your own work, it's best to hire a professional.

CAMERAS

Polaroid, single lens reflex, and digital cameras are useful for shooting photographic reference images for projects and for recording the status of a piece as it progresses. With e-mail and faxes, I keep my clients up-to-date by sending them images at different stages of a project. Once I complete an image, I have it shot by a professional photographer. Since my images are mainly used for publication and advertisements, they are photographed as 8"-x-10" or 4"-x-5" chromes.

LIGHT BOX

A light box is useful for tracing your pattern onto fabrics. It allows you to see your pattern's lines through the fabric so you can trace the shapes accurately.

It is a rectangular box, usually made of wood, with a top surface (of glass or Plexiglas) that is translucent. There is an electric light source inside the box and an on/off switch. Light boxes are available in a variety of sizes through catalogs and at art stores and quilt supply stores. (I would suggest a light box that is 12" x 19" or larger in order to accommodate the size of your pattern.)

If you do not want to purchase one, you can create a makeshift light box by putting a small lamp in a box or laundry basket with a piece of glass (or Plexiglas) attached to the top of the basket. A piece of tracing paper taped to the underside of the glass will diffuse and even out the lighting. (However, make sure that there is adequate ventilation so that the lightbulb's heat does not build up and cause a fire.)

LIGHTING

Although it's sensible to have efficient lighting everywhere in your workplace, it is especially important to have good lighting at your sewing machine area, because of the nature of the close work. In my case, I make use of the built-in light on my sewing machine, plus a high-intensity light aimed at the needle area and a drafting-table light that shines on the project.

My mother always suggested that, to reduce eyestrain while doing detail-oriented work, you should occasionally raise your eyes and look out the window or off toward the distance. I do this, and it works for me.

I take my own photographs to use for reference. In the lower right corner are four photographs of artist Charlene Tarbox, who posed for my image "Four Seasons."

"Four Seasons," 14" x 11" (1983), was used on the cover of *Meetings and Conventions* Magazine and later on the cover of *Reader's Digest* Magazine. Commissioned by Northstar Travel Media

Storage

It's been important to me, all my life as an artist, to have a place to work. As a child, it was the dining-room table, then a corner of my older sister Pat's basement studio at our parents' house, and then an over-sized worktable in what was my very small bedroom. As an adult, I had the experience of working in communal spaces at college and then sharing space with roommates.

In 1973 my husband, Frank, and I bought a four-story Brooklyn brownstone. After "migrating" from two other studios within our house, I now have an entire floor, 21' x 37', for my current studio. We commissioned an architect to design it, including built-in shelving and much of the storage areas. Later, I added file cabinets, bookshelves, and other storage units (most of which were second-hand or tag sale items). I also use two closets and the cellar for storage. Even though that is a lot of space, I have already filled it up. My explanation to Frank is that my ancestors were farmers and that what I really need is a large barn to store all of my stuff.

There are two kinds of people in this world: packrats, and people who like to get rid of things. Frank, who falls into the second category, will tell you that I am definitely a packrat. This has been both a blessing and a curse.

The blessing is that when I have a commission with a deadline looming, I usually don't have to go outside of my studio to find all the supplies I need to complete the project. Over the years I have stocked up on art supplies and office supplies. And that goes for fabric as well.

The two-pronged curse of this bounty is that it is a bit daunting to organize these supplies, and they also take up a lot of room. But it is truly wonderful to reach for, and find, that particular blue fabric that I know would be perfect for the lake in a landscape that I might be working

on, or to know that I have a multiplicity of skin tones in my boxes of flesh-colored fabrics.

The following sections deal with organizing and storing your materials and supplies—the fabrics, notions, art supplies, reference materials, etc.—that will go into the creation of your fabric artwork.

FABRIC STORAGE

If I purchased the fabric on a roll, I wrap it in brown paper and/or a plastic sleeve to protect the fabric from dust and light. However, most of my fabric is enclosed in plastic bags and stored in boxes on my studio's shelves.

What has worked for me is built-in shelves that accommodate corrugated boxes that are approximately 14" x 14" x 14". I order the boxes from an office supply company, so that they will be uniform in size. I cover the front of each box with white Con-Tact® adhesive covering. The white boxes blend in with the white walls of my studio, and this keeps my workplace from looking cluttered. I put a heavy-duty, 30-gallon plastic bag inside each box to hold that box's fabric. Some people neatly fold their fabric before storing it; however, I am not that compulsive about my collection. My fabric is *not* folded; it's merely "mushed" together in the bags.

I categorize the fabrics primarily by color. However, since I have so much fabric, it takes several boxes to cover a range of value of each color. For example, with brown fabric, one box holds my beige fabric; another, my tan fabric; another, my light brown fabric; another, my brown fabric; and one last box holds my dark brown fabric. And I have more than ten boxes that hold different variations of white fabric!

Besides sorting my fabrics according to color, I also have separate boxes for

Each area of my fabric storage has a diagram that shows the color of the fabric that is in each storage box.

My checkerboard fabrics are stored in two boxes categorized by "warm" and "cool." This helps me find the exact fabric I am seeking when I am in the midst of a project, such as "Self-Portrait in Checkerboard" shown in detail below.

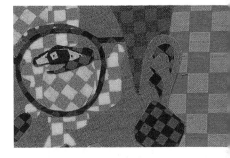

A variety of checkerboard fabrics were used in this self-portrait. (The complete artwork is pictured on page 55.)

fabrics that are brocades, florals, calicos, striped, nostalgic, lacy, sheer, polka dots, checkerboard, ethnic, etc.

I also use "warm" (yellow, orange, red, brown, white) and "cool" (blue, green, purple, black) as categories for printed or brocade fabrics. For instance, I have a box of warm-colored striped fabric and another box for cool-colored striped fabric.

Because I like to experiment with checkerboard and polka dot fabrics, I have assembled a palette of colors and variations of these fabrics: several boxes devoted to "large checkerboard fabrics in warm tones of color," "small checkerboard fabrics in cool tones of color," and the like.

I keep my fabric out of sight because I do not like to be distracted by seeing all of it all the time. And I don't label the boxes, because I like the plain white surface and I would find it distracting to have labels. Visitors to my studio always ask, "How do you know what is in each box?" My answer is that I have a basic sense of what fabrics I have on hand and that I also keep a diagram positioned near each storage area. The diagrams list what color fabric is in each box and where that box is located in relation to the others.

This system works for me—with the large volume of fabric that I've accumulated—and it may be useful for you in organizing your fabric collection. However, there may be other solutions that work even better. Experiment until you find what suits you best. In the end, having a system to sort and organize your fabric will make locating the best fabric choices for your projects easier and faster.

NOTIONS STORAGE

To store buttons, embroidery thread, and trimmings, I first sort these items by color into individual plastic bags and then assemble them in plastic storage drawers. This kind of organizing takes time initially, but it makes it a lot easier to find that "certain something" that truly enhances a project.

It helps to keep pencils, staplers, and scissors near the phone and at the areas where I draw, work on slides, do my correspondence, etc.

Canvas stretchers, in a variety of sizes, are stored in a cabinet.

The spools of sewing machine thread are organized by color and stored in drawers.

THREAD STORAGE

My spools of sewing machine thread are stored in drawers (salvaged from a retired cruise ship) within easy reach of my sewing machine.

I sort the threads according to color and value (how light or dark the color is). This organization makes it simple to find the exact thread colors to match each project's fabrics.

Skeins of embroidery thread are sorted according to color and stored in smaller bags. These bags are then stored in large plastic bags based on the specific shades of color.

ART SUPPLY STORAGE

Since my studio is fairly large and since I like to keep pencils, staplers, and scissors nearby, I have several stations at the various tables and counters in my studio where these materials are available whenever I need them.

CANVAS STRETCHER STORAGE

Canvas stretchers can be bought in a variety of sizes. I use rubber bands to sort the stretchers into pairs and store the stretchers in a cabinet. I keep a chart that lists the sizes that I have on hand.

Within the flat files I store printed images in acetate sleeves, organized by category, making it easier to locate them.

PAPER STORAGE

My tear sheets (printed images of my stitched illustration work that were used in magazines, posters, etc.) as well as my paper supplies (tracing paper, acetate, etc.) are kept in metal flat files, which are able to safely store a lot of material. The tear sheets are organized according to subject matter: landscapes, people, dimensional, etc.

SLIDE STORAGE

To document my stitched artwork, I have it professionally photographed as 8"-x-10" transparencies, which are later made into slides. The slides are stored in metal storage drawers and organized by general categories: cityscapes, still lifes, people, etc. Within each category they are alphabetized by title. I use the slides when submitting my work to new clients and/or to competitions.

INFORMATION STORAGE

Rolodex Filing System Some people use computers to store all of their information. However, being somewhat old-fashioned (and since I don't always have my computer turned on), I use Rolodex cards to store all sorts of information, such as phone numbers of clients and other artists, and sources for supplies, etc. I also use them to list the amount of time a project took (this is helpful in pricing future commissions) and to keep notes on procedures developed for specific projects. I use an individual Rolodex card for each piece of information.

The cards are organized into general categories: For example, all of the fabric stores are listed under "Fabric," ribbon stores are listed under "Trimmings," and the like. Artist friends have dubbed me the "Networking Queen of Brooklyn" because I can readily answer their questions—by finding the information on my old-fashioned Rolodex cards.

Photo Reference Sources and Filing System It is possible to research and find images on the Internet and in commercial photo references services, as well as at some public libraries. However, I have found that it's also useful to keep a file of images on hand for inspiration. I have hundreds and hundreds of photos (cut from magazines, greeting cards, etc.) that are stored in several file drawers in my studio. They are organized alphabetically by categories: animals, architecture, birds, butterflies, boats, etc. These are invaluable when I am starting a project. (For more information on using photo references and copyright infringement issues, see pages 34–35.)

(For more information on using photo references and copyright infringement issues, see pages 34–35.)

> **HINT**
> Wooden flat files, though they are more attractive, might leach oil or chemicals onto whatever you store in the drawers. Metal flat files are preferable.

My Rolodex filing system has been useful for storing information.

SAFETY IN THE FABRIC STUDIO by Monona Rossol

Please note that the following advice is for artists who work alone in their studios. You must take additional precautions, which are not detailed here, if you teach in your studio or share your space with other artists, or if you employ workers, even one part-time employee.

MATERIALS-HANDLING PRECAUTIONS

The hazards involved in fabric work include exposure to fabric dust, molds, paints and adhesive sprays, dyes, and repetitive strain injuries. But you can easily mitigate most of them with simple precautions.

For centuries, serious respiratory diseases have been associated with *dust from natural fibers* such as cotton, hemp, sisal, jute, and flax. But the fibers are not very hazardous after they are milled into textiles. Synthetic fiber dusts from rayon, acetate, nylon, and acrylic fibers have also been found to cause lung irritation. Nylon flocking fibers, in particular, cause a disabling illness called interstitial lung disease. Keeping the studio clean and avoiding inhalation of fabric dusts provides protection.

Fiber treatments such as permanent press, sizing, or fire retardant chemicals are associated with diseases in workers in textile retail outlets. For example, formaldehyde is emitted by certain permanent press treatment chemicals. A well-ventilated studio should eliminate this hazard.

Naphthalene and paradichlorobenzene, two chemicals commonly used for *mothproofing and mothballs*, are toxic and suspected of causing cancer. Mothballs usually are not needed if good storage methods are used and inventories are inspected regularly.

Many *dyes* break down to release cancer-causing substances in the body. For this reason, the German government has banned such dyes for use on fabrics intended for contact with the human body, such as clothing and bed linens. Other European countries are following Germany's lead. However, these dyes are not banned in the United States. Worse, fabric artists usually cannot even find out if the fabrics they use contain them. But controlling fabric dust and avoiding use of fabrics whose dyes come off on hands or run excessively in wash water are good practices.

Toxic *pigments* are used in acrylics, watercolors, and fabric paints. The pigments will not get into your body if you do not airbrush or spray the paints, heat or sand them, or eat or drink while you work.

Spray adhesives and solvent-based markers contain toxic *solvents*. Ordinary ventilation should be sufficient for occasional use of marking pens. But aerosol sprays should be used outdoors or in a spray booth (see page 25 for more details).

Ironing releases by-products from dyes, fabric treatments, and plastic decomposition chemicals from spray adhesives and fusible webbing. You can smell these chemicals. Some of them are known to be hazardous, but the amounts released are unknown. Prudence dictates that good ventilation should be provided during ironing.

Take care when using spray adhesive.

Molds can grow on textiles. Molds can cause irritation of eyes and respiratory system, allergies, and infections. Some are also toxic. Molds cannot thrive if the studio's temperature and humidity are controlled and if water sources such as leaks and flooding are addressed immediately.

THE SAFE STUDIO

Floors, surfaces, and storage units should be made of materials that are easily mopped and sponged clean.

Proper *ventilation* is essential. While window air-conditioners can keep most small studios comfortable, these units draw air from the room, cool it, and blow the same air out again. As such, air-conditioners alone do not provide sufficient fresh air for a healthy studio. Fresh air can be provided by open windows in small studios. Larger studios need ventilation systems designed by mechanical engineers.

Sprays and airbrush products should be used outdoors or in a spray booth. If you use a spray booth, note that fire codes usually require that it be explosion proof and that all electrical lights, switches, and fixtures within 10' of the face of a booth are also explosion proof. This can be costly. Other special ventilation systems that may be needed include range hoods over stoves (if you do hot dye application or dye stripping, etc.), window exhaust fans for rapid studio air exchange (if you work with solvents in amounts that a dilution vent is needed periodically), or venting for washers and dryers.

Self-employed artists do not come under workplace regulations, but artists should know that these laws prohibit workers from wearing toxic *dust masks or respirators* until they have:

- a medical professional's certification that they have no physical condition that would be worsened by breathing stress;
- fit testing done by a person trained in one of the approved test methods; and
- training in use, maintenance, and limitations.

These services are only available to individuals through occupational clinics and consultants at significant costs. Without them, however, respirators may only be providing a false sense of security. For nontoxic dusts, a single-strap pollen mask from the drugstore can be used. Toxic dusts, vapors, and gases will go through these masks.

General safety equipment for the studio should include first-aid supplies for needle sticks and small cuts, fire extinguishers, smoke detectors, and protective gloves and eyewear if needed.

Material Safety Data Sheets (MSDSs) on all paints, sprays, and toxic products should be obtained and filed, and their advice followed. (Manufacturers should provide MSDSs at no cost.)

Ergonomic injuries from hours of intense, detailed work can include various types of muscle and nerve damage. Purchase a *chair* that can be adjusted to a height at which your arms are in a relaxed, comfortable position when you work. If your hands or arms tingle or ache for prolonged periods, consult a physician.

Always provide enough *light* for the tasks you do. Although there are standards for the amount of light needed for close work, your own eyes are usually the best instrument for detecting when you are straining to do the work.

The most important piece of equipment you own is your *body*. Get plenty of rest, food, exercise, and enjoyment from your work.

MONONA ROSSOL is president of Arts, Crafts & Theater Safety and is a renowned industrial hygienist expert.

SPRAY BOOTHS

What Are They? A spray booth is a device whose fan draws spray mists into an enclosure, pulls the mists through a filter to capture the solid parts (e.g., pigments, adhesives), draws the solvents from the mist (in a vapor form) through ductwork, and exhausts the solvent vapors to the outside air. There are a few types of spray booths that trap the solvent vapors in large charcoal filters instead of releasing them outdoors. These are not recommended unless the amounts of solvents you use have been estimated and are known not to quickly exceed the capacity of the filter so fast that frequent changing of those expensive filters is needed. Also not recommended are the items called "spray booths" that are sold in some magazines and catalogs which are either empty boxes into which spraying is done or which have a fan that exhausts the solvent vapors back into the room.

Choosing the Booth Searching for "spray booths" on the Internet should result in a number of sources. The manufacturers and distributors can suggest which of their products they recommend once you tell them exactly what your sprays contain and how often you expect to spray. You should

also tell them about any other processes you may want to do in the booth, such as sanding or mixing dye powders. When you have found a booth that appears to meet your needs, check the equipment's specifications with a local mechanical engineer or industrial hygienist. Never rely totally on the seller for advice. The local engineer or industrial hygienist can determine if the booth has the special features needed to meet local codes and to prevent fires and explosions from the solvent vapors.

Installing the Booth Good spray booth companies will also install the spray booth. But you will still need your local experts to be certain that the installation will meet local codes. Usually, spray booths must be a significant distance away from sources of ordinary electrical equipment, sources of heat, flames, etc. There may even be codes dictating the location of the booth's exhaust or regulations that require a permit.

While all this seems like a lot of trouble, the result is that your workplace will have a safe place to use toxic and flammable materials.

Cityscapes

Though I've enjoyed many rural countrysides, I've spent most of my life in cities: Chicago, where I was born, and New York City, where I've lived for most of my life.

I'm always fascinated with the texture and color of cities—both the skyscrapers of Manhattan and the brownstones of Boerum Hill, our Brooklyn neighbor-hood. As I do errands or travel to appointments, I make mental notes of how sunlight hits the buildings and defines their shapes and also how trees can soften a cityscape's hard surfaces. (To see the kinds of buildings where I live, see "Town and Country," on page 52, "Fulton Street Mall," on page 53, and "Golden Opportunity," on facing page.)

While You're Sleeping
15" x 11" (2001)
Artwork for "While You're Sleeping" first appeared on the cover of the September 2001 issue of CLICK magazine published by Carus Publishing Company.

"Architecture is frozen music."
JOHANN WOLFGANG
VAN GOETHE

Altman's
19" x 19" (1981)
Commissioned by Altman's Department Store for catalog cover. Collection of Nancy Cogen.

St. Louis
16" x 16" (1995)
Commissioned by and Collection of St. John's Hospital.

New York, New York
20" x 96" (2002)
Commissioned by and Collection of Kam and Walter Chin.

New York Is Book Country
24¹/₄" x 18¹/₄" (1997)
New York Is Book Country Street Fair Poster 1997

Golden Opportunity
16" x 15" (1986)
Commissioned by Consumers Digest for *Money Maker* Magazine

O Come All Ye Faithful
20" x 16¹/₄" (1983)
Commissioned by Harcourt, Brace, Jovanovich, Inc. for *The Christmas Carol Sampler*

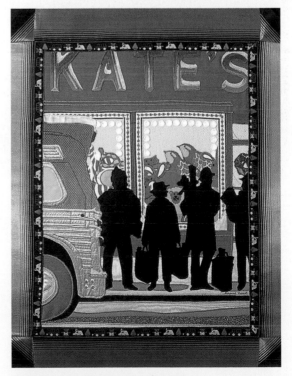

God Rest Ye Merry Gentlemen
27¹/₄" x 22¹/₄" (1983)
Commissioned by Harcourt, Brace, Jovanovich, Inc. for *The Christmas Carol Sampler*

CHAPTER 2

Designing Your Pattern

Americas farmland is the tongue-in-cheek theme of "Down on the Farm." My grandparents, on both sides of my family, were farmers, so even though I have never lived on a farm, I must have some "farming genes" in my blood. "Down on the Farm," which you can see on page 38, was commissioned as a cover for a country music album. When I received the assignment, I felt that it was an opportunity to make a colorful, idealized image of farm life. Having lived in cities all my life, I decided to make use of all that said "country" to me. Therefore, I included a farmhouse, barn, animals, windmill, silo, rolling hills, the American flag, a girl in overalls, Dad, Mom, and even an apple pie!

The instructions in this chapter will help you create stitched artwork patterns. I've also included information on design and composition, using "Down on the Farm" as an example of these techniques. In Chapter 3, you can create your own artwork based on the pattern you make in this chapter or make your own version of this image.

"Down on the Farm" begins with a sketch that
eventually becomes the pattern.

Designing the Pattern

GENERAL MATERIALS NEEDED
❧

tracing paper pad, 24" x 18"
(*optional*: vellum or acetate)

pencils

acetate, 18" x 24"
(*optional*)

transparency film, 8¹/₂" x 11"
(made for making overhead projector transparencies copies)

Pigma Micron pen
(black)

artist's white tape

Stabilo pencils
(white, black, yellow, and red)

light box
(*optional*)
❧

NOTE The General Materials Needed list above is a listing of the materials that are used to make each of the **patterns** in this book. Additional materials needed for specific projects are listed in each chapter.

STEP 1
DESIGNING YOUR IMAGE

When creating your drawing, which will later become your pattern, think about what you want to accomplish with your project. Write down your thoughts, cut out pictures from magazines, bookmark images in art books, download images from the Internet. You can also do rough sketches of your concepts (see photo above right on facing page).

You might base your fabric artwork on a variety of sources:

- your own sketches
- images from magazines, newspapers, etc. (before proceeding, see "Copyright Ins and Outs" on pages 34 to 35)
- photographs

If you work from *your own sketches*, I suggest that you do a number of "thumbnail sketches," which are postcard-sized (or smaller) drawings of your concepts. Then consider all your sketches and choose your favorite. Enlarge this sketch to the final size that you wish to work in. Refine the sketch in pencil on tracing paper or vellum. Use a pencil at this stage so you can make erasures and adjustments to your sketch more easily. If need be, draw and redraw areas of your sketch onto small pieces of tracing paper. Move the pieces around on top of the drawing and tape them down when you are satisfied with the way it looks. Then trace these areas onto the drawing. (In Chapter 3, Step 4, when you put the drawing on a light box with fabric on top of it, the transparency of the tracing paper will make it possible for you to trace your lines directly onto the fabric.)

You may decide to create your drawing using a *compilation of images from magazines and newspapers*. If so, put tracing paper over your chosen images and trace the outline of the shapes. Make adjustments

To create the sketch of the farmhouse, I considered many images from my reference files.

to the shapes as you wish and enlarge your sketches to the size that you need for your drawing using a copier machine. Move the tracing paper pieces around until you are satisfied with the composition. (If you need a mirror image of your sketch or of part of it, turn the tracing paper over to the other side and you will have the mirror image of the front.)

"Make a drawing; begin it again; trace it; begin it again and trace it again."
EDGAR DEGAS

If you decide to create your drawing based on a *photograph*, enlarge it to the size that you need for your drawing. Cover the enlargement with tracing paper and create a line drawing version of it by tracing the shapes.

Also keep in mind that your drawing should be made up not just of lines but of complete shapes, and that these shapes will later be cut out of fabric. So when creating your drawing, decide on how these final shapes will look. For example, in drawing a face, if you draw an area that is meant to look as if it is in shadows, that area cannot be indicated by an incomplete line; it must be drawn as a complete shape so the corresponding fabric shape can be cut out later.

Even after following all of the suggestions above, sometimes it's helpful to take a break from your drawing before finalizing it. So at this point, have a cup of tea or run an errand. When you return and look at your drawing with fresh eyes, you may change your mind about it. If that is the case, make any last-minute changes to finalize the drawing. (If you are creating a portrait, see Step 3 on page 99 for more information on how to create shapes in faces.)

I created several thumbnail sketches before deciding on a direction for "Down on the Farm."

The drawing is initially created in pencil.

HINT
Drawings that are based too closely on photographs sometimes end up looking awkward because photographs include harsh shadows. Also, the angle in which the photograph was taken may present awkward foreshortening. (To show what I mean by foreshortening: Stand in front of a mirror and extend your arm toward it. You will see that if you were to draw what you see in the mirror, your extended arm would be rather awkward looking.) My suggestion for improving your drawing is to make adjustments to the traced photograph. Keep drawing and redrawing it until you are pleased with the results.

COMPOSITION

The word *composition* is defined as "the act of combining parts or elements to form a whole." Most people have an intuitive sense of composition. If you have ever arranged your living-room furniture, organized a letter on a computer, or set a festive holiday table, you already have a basic knowledge of composition. Nonetheless, to give yourself more confidence, my advice is: Read books and take art classes to hone your skills in composition and drawing. Try analyzing artwork and photographs that you admire. Put a piece of tracing paper over a copy of a painting you love, roughly trace the elements, and see what makes it "work." When you look at artwork, be aware of its important parts: What is the route that your eyes take? Where did the artist want you to focus your attention?

Following are a few tips on composition to help you with your sketches.

Balance A good composition has its own sense of balance. However, it's not simply a matter of having an equal number of items on each side.

Look at your drawing. Just for a moment, pretend that each of the elements in it had a weight. With that in mind, would one side of your drawing "tip over" because it was much heavier than the other side? If so, try rearranging the elements, making some larger or smaller.

Recropping your image is another possibility. (See page 98 for information on how to make "croppers" to help you decide on the final size and shape of your drawing.)

"Begin by determining your composition. Then the values—the relation of the forms to the values. These are the basics. Then the color, and finally the finish."
JEAN-BAPTIST-CAMILLE COROT

Division of Space There are many ways to approach composition. In Western art, perspective and visual clues are helpful. In Asian art, space is implied by creating overlap and positioning elements higher in the composition to let the viewer know that these elements are farther away. In folk art traditions, overlap is purposefully avoided. This creates an ambiguity of space and creates an off-kilter sense of space, which adds to folk art's charm.

Focus Ask yourself: "What's the most important element in this drawing? How do I want the viewer's eye to get there?" By making the important part of your drawing larger, simpler, or more colorful, you will divert the viewer's focus there. Experiment with different versions of your composition to see what works best. Use tracing paper or a copier machine to make several copies of your drawing. Make alterations to each and then choose one that works best.

Overlapping one element over the next will lead the viewer through your drawing. Diagonal lines will also help the viewer navigate through your composition.

Since the focus of "Country Celebration," 22" x 29" (1986), is on the people of all nationalities in the foreground at the table, I devoted only about a third of the image to the sky.
Commissioned by North American Mission Board (formerly Home Mission Board)

HINT
With landscapes, it's sometimes helpful to divide your composition into three horizontal sections and devote two-thirds of your space either to land or to sky.

STEP 2
DRAWING THE SHAPES

Once your drawing is complete, go over all the pencil lines with a black Pentel marker (see diagram below). Or, if you like, darken the lines by using a copier machine on a dark setting and printing your drawing onto an 8 1/2"-x-11" acetate. (If the size of your drawing is larger than 8 1/2" x 11", use several acetate sheets. Print the drawing in sections and attach them together with cellophane tape.) Make sure that the acetate's printed lines are dark. When you use a light box to trace the shapes onto fabric in Chapter 3, Step 4, the lines have to be dark enough so you can see them through your fabrics.

Now that you've made the lines of your drawing dark enough, we'll call this your *pattern*—a transparent version of your drawing, in the size that you envision for your finished fabric artwork.

Next, make two paper copies of the pattern at 50 percent reduction. These small copies will be used in Chapter 3, Step 2, when you create your rough fabric paste-up and continue with the steps that will transform your pattern into an appliquéd artwork.

HINT
Use only acetate meant for opaque projector presentations. If you use other types of acetate, the heat of the copier machine may melt the acetate and ruin the copier.

Use a Pentel marker to darken the lines. This will make it easier to trace them onto your fabric in Chapter 3, Step 4.

COPYRIGHT INS AND OUTS by Tad Crawford

You may already have some knowledge about copyright, but lawyer and publisher Tad Crawford gives you a great deal of information about this valuable protection for artists.

Copyright protects you from having your art stolen by someone else. As the copyright owner, you may either allow or prevent someone else from publishing or making derivations of your work (such as a painting based on a fabric design of your creation). Your copyrights last for *your lifetime plus another seventy years*, so a successful work may benefit not only you, but your heirs as well. Make sure you don't sign a work-for-hire contract or assign all rights to your art, because then the commissioning party, *not you,* will own the copyright and gain its benefits.

LICENSING RIGHTS

To license any exclusive right of copyright (which means *only the licensee* can do what the license stipulates), you, or your authorized agent, must sign a written license. If no written license is signed, then the usage can, at most, be nonexclusive, which allows you to license the same usage to more than one party. You should license only *limited* rights of usage in your copyrights, limiting the rights by type of product or medium, duration of use, and territory of use (including whether the image can be used on the Web). All rights not licensed should be retained by you as the creator. After the description of what rights are licensed, your contract should state, "Any usage rights not explicitly licensed hereunder are reserved to the artist."

REGISTRATION

You don't have to register your art to obtain a copyright, because federal law gives you the copyright from the moment you create a work. However, registration with the Copyright Office will help you in the event your work is infringed upon. You can obtain Copyright Application Form VA (for Visual Art) by writing to the Copyright Office, Library of Congress, Washington, D.C. 20559; calling at 202 707-9100; or downloading off their Web site at www.copyright.gov/. The Copyright Office has numerous helpful circulars that can be requested or downloaded from the Web site.

COPYRIGHT NOTICE

It is no longer necessary to place copyright notice either on unpublished or published works of art. Since March 1, 1989, the absence of copyright notice cannot cause the loss of the copyright. However, the lack of notice may give infringers a loophole to try and lessen their damages. So it is still wise to place copyright notice on your works (especially when published) as a visible symbol of your rights as copyright owner.

Copyright notice has three elements: (1) "Copyright" or "Copr" or "©"; (2) your name; and (3) the year of first publication.

INFRINGEMENT

Your work is infringed when someone uses it without your authorization. The test for infringement is whether an ordinary observer would believe one work was copied from another. The damages for infringement are the actual losses of the person whose work is infringed plus any profits of the infringer. In some cases (especially if the work was registered before the infringement), the court can simply award an amount between $750 and $30,000 for each work infringed. If the infringement is willful, this amount can be increased to as much as $150,000. Contrary to the beliefs of some Internet enthusiasts, copyright laws *do* apply to the Internet, and unauthorized use of art from a Web site is an infringement.

To maximize your position with respect to infringers, it is always wise to register all your fabric art, especially work that you think is a likely target for infringers. Also, if you can't afford to hire a lawyer to bring an expensive copyright lawsuit, you might be eligible to use one of the many volunteer lawyers for the arts groups across the country. You can contact the Volunteer Lawyers for the Arts in New York City (1 East 53 Street, New York, New York 10022; 212 319-2787; www.vlany.org) to find the group closest to you.

If you use someone else's copyrighted work without his or her permission, you always run the risk of infringing that person's copyright. As stated before, this is true for art that you may find on the Web, as well as art from other sources. The test for infringement is whether an ordinary observer believes your work to be copied from the other person's work. If you change the work to such a degree that an ordinary observer will not see any copying—such as by altering the original work and adding new designs to it—you will be safe. Keep in mind that there is no percentage test—such as changing 25 percent or 50 percent of the original work—that will guarantee you have changed the original work enough. Also, in some cases your copying will be obvious, but it still may not be an infringement because it is what is called a "fair use."

FAIR USE

A fair use is a use of someone else's work that is allowed under the copyright law. Four factors are used to determine whether using all or part of another artist's work is a fair use: (1) the purpose and character of the use, including whether or not it is for profit; (2) the character of the copyrighted work (if it is news or factual, fair use is more likely to be found, whereas using fantasy or entertaining works makes a finding of fair use less likely; (3) how much of the total work is used in the course of the use; and (4) what effect the use will have on the market for or value of the copyrighted work. If you want to avoid potential copyright infringements, you can seek written permission from the person who created the art that you are copying. If you receive permission, you would then be a licensee with the right to create and sell images of that art.

PUBLIC DOMAIN
Since copyright is for a limited term, after the copyright term has ended, art becomes part of the public domain. Works in the public domain may be freely copied by anyone. Works published in the United States in 1922 or earlier are in the public domain in the United States. Later works might also be in the public domain but would have to be reviewed on a case-by-case basis.

PERMISSIONS
To obtain permission to publish works that are not in the public domain and cannot be used as a fair use, you should send the copyright holder a simple permission form. This would set forth what kind of fabric artwork you are doing, what images (or words) you want to use, what rights you need to the material, what credit line and copyright notice will be given, and what payment you will make to him or her. If it is agreeable to the copyright holder, he or she will sign the permission form. *Legal Guide for the Visual Artist* (Allworth Press, 2001) has an appropriate permission form.

CELEBRITIES
The copyright law does not deal with the issue of whether images of celebrities can be used in art. However, the question is often raised, so we will review the various issues here. It helps to distinguish between copyright, which protects the right to make copies or derivations of a work, and privacy or publicity rights,

which protect the images of people. If you are copying the images of rock stars or movie stars, you may be committing a copyright infringement unless your use is a fair use or you have obtained permission from the artist or photographer who made the original image. For the copyright violation, you would risk being sued. However, living people also have a right of privacy. You cannot use anyone's image for purposes of advertising or trade (such as using the image on tee shirts) without that person's permission (which you should always get in writing, as a number of states require, in any event). A public figure loses his or her right of privacy with respect to newsworthy information but *not* with respect to advertising or trade uses. In fact, a famous person gains what is called the *right of publicity*, which is the right to profit from the exploitation of his or her name or image for purposes of advertising or trade. By court decisions and laws in a number of states, this right of publicity actually can survive death for as long as fifty years in some states. While some laws exempt single or original works of fine art, art in multiples is likely to be distributed nationally and be subject to the most restrictive of these so-called celebrity rights laws. Permission may be requested directly from the celebrity or, more likely, from the celebrity's agent. While the right of privacy protects only living people, the right of publicity may also protect deceased celebrities. In such a case, permission will have to be sought from the celebrity's estate or the agent for the estate.

"The United States of America," 29" x 43" (1984), was created for American Express for use as a promotional poster. The client purchased the copyright and all the rights to the image. However, when I requested the right to license the image for use on puzzles and other products, the client agreed.
Commissioned by and Collection of American Express Co., Inc.

TAD CRAWFORD **is an attorney, publisher, author of** *Legal Guide for the Visual Artist,* **Business and** *Legal Forms for Fine Artists,* **and** *The Artist-Gallery Partnership* **(all published by Allworth Press). More information about his books and other books to help artists can be found at the Allworth Press Web site: http://www.allworth.com/Pages/SC_AC**

Landscapes

It might be said that I've never met a landscape artist that I didn't like—Grandma Moses, Paul Cezanne, Grant Wood, Henri Rousseau. They're all different in their approach, but they all have had an influence on how I see landscapes. When I made my first drawing as a child (which consisted of a typical house, grass, sky, clouds, and yellow sun), I knew that landscapes would present a wealth of opportunities to explore.

City and Country Landscape
15¹/₂" x 25¹/₂" (1995)
Commissioned by Harcourt, Inc. Reproduced by permission of the publisher.

"The big artist keeps an eye on nature and steals her tools."
THOMAS EAKINS

Small Towns, Time Magazine cover
14⁵/₈" x 11" (1997)
Commissioned by Time Inc. for 12/8/97 cover. TIME and the Red Border are registered trademarks of Time Inc. © 1997 Time Inc. Used with Permission.

Main Street, USA
17" x 16 " (2001)
Commissioned by Time Inc. for *TIME FOR KIDS* Magazine

My Creek
13" x 17" (1980)
Commissioned by G+J USA Publishing for *Parents* Magazine. Private collection.

Peaceful Landscape
17" x 14"
Commissioned for *America West* Magazine. Collection of Harriet and Alvin Sigal.

Perrier
27" x 20" (1978)
The PERRIER ad is copyrighted by Nestle Waters North America, used with its permission. Collection of Hal Goluboff.

Shenandoah
30" x 20" (1975)
Commissioned for "Shenandoah," Broadway musical poster. Collection of Philip Rose and Doris Belack.

House and Family
16¹/2" x 15" (1986)
Commissioned by and Collection of Roxane Laboratories, Inc.

CHAPTER 3

Creating Your Artwork

This chapter will show you how to turn a pattern into finished stitched artwork. If you designed your own pattern in Chapter 2, use it and this chapter's step-by-step instructions to complete your project.

If you wish to make your own version of "Down on the Farm," enlarge the pattern that appears on page 114 and follow the instructions that begin on the next page.

Either way, have fun.

Down on the Farm
20" x 20" (1988)
Commissioned by *Reader's Digest Music*
for "God Bless the U.S.A." record cover

Stitching "Down on the Farm"

GENERAL MATERIALS NEEDED

white cotton duck fabric, 1 yard
(used for backing)
(NOTE Add 1¹/₂" of extra fabric on all sides to the size of your pattern)

lightweight white batiste fabric, 1 yard
(used for backing in overall padding technique, which is further explained in Chapter 7) (optional)

white felt
(used for selective padding technique, which is further explained in Chapter 6) (optional)

lightweight batting, 1 yard
(used for overall padding technique, which is further explained in Chapter 7) (optional)

paper-backed fusible webbing

pressing cloth
(use sheer cotton fabric for ironing)

thread

trimmings ribbons
(optional)

cardboard, 2 pieces, each 18" x 24"

3M Spraymount adhesive

canvas stretchers or foam core
(optional)

tweezers
(optional)

To create "Down on the Farm" you will also need:

your pattern

fabrics of your choice

Materials
is a listing of
are used to
projects in
al materials
projects are
ter.

STEP 1
CHOOSING FABRICS

Since my method involves ironing fusible webbing onto the back of fabrics, there are very few limitations on the *kinds* of fabric that can be used. Nonetheless, when you choose your fabrics, consider how they relate to one another: whether the fabrics are lightweight or bulky, transparent or opaque; and how the colors and prints work together. You may be interested in bold contrast and bright colors for one project yet at another time want to create a project that calls for fabrics that are subtler or closer in value.

When I start a project, I usually have a color scheme in mind. To me, color has a personality and transmits emotion, mood, and even a sense of time. So I go to my fabric collection with a general notion of the kinds of colors that I'm seeking.

I start by pulling out boxes of fabric and dumping the contents out on the floor, so I can get at the pieces that will add up to the final "look" that I'm after. At this stage, with the piled fabric all around me, I choose any and all that are of interest to me. In some cases, I pick four or five fabrics as possibilities for what may be just a small shape in the finished fabric artwork. Then I narrow down my choices to the specific fabrics that "speak to me," and I start to assemble a palette of fabrics—keeping color, pattern, and texture in mind while considering how the fabrics relate to one another.

So, don't be afraid to be messy. Choose your fabrics and assemble them in piles on your worktable. Start with the fabric for the most important shape and proceed from there, until you have made all of your choices.

CONSIDERING VALUE IN YOUR FABRIC CHOICES

Value relates to the lightness and darkness of the fabric's colors. In other words, if all of your colored fabrics were translated into black, white, and gray, which fabrics would be darker and which would be lighter? Which would be more dominant? Which ones would be more compatible and similar to the others? How would the fabrics relate to one another?

For certain projects you might want to choose colors that are similar in value. For others you might want fabrics that have a wide range of values. You should decide what works best for each project. A lot of these decisions are intuitive, but experimentation is very helpful.

Keep in mind the values of the colors and how they contrast and/or work with one another.

COLOR

There are many books and art classes on Color Theory. Reading these books and taking classes is beneficial and raises your awareness of color. However, you, like most people, have an innate sense of color, and you should feel confident enough to trust your own sense of "what goes well with what." Below are a few exercises for experimenting with your own sense of color.

Use the simple drawing of "Landscape," pictured below, as the basis for five of your own fabric landscapes. Enlarge the drawing to 8" x 6" and make five copies of it for the following exercises. The results of these exercises are not necessarily meant to be sewn or completed. They are just experiments in color. For each exercise, follow the instructions. Choose your colors and fabrics. Create a rough fabric paste-up landscape by cutting out fabric shapes and taping them onto your paper copy. (As mentioned in Chapter 1, a rough fabric paste-up is a collage of selected fabrics, glued or taped down in the same positions as they will be in a finished artwork. For help in making rough fabric paste-ups, see the instructions on page 42.)

Exercise 1 Use your favorite color (plus several colors that you think will work well with it). Consider using the colors of the clothes that you are wearing today.

Exercise 2 Use your least favorite color (plus whatever colors that you think will enhance it and make it look more appealing).

Exercise 3 Analyze a classic painting from a museum or art book and note what colors were used. Do a rough fabric paste-up of the "Landscape" using only those colors that were in the painting.

Exercise 4 Look out your window in the early morning and make a note of the colors that you see. Find matching colors in fabric or paper and do a rough fabric paste-up of the "Landscape" using those colors.

Exercise 5 Look at the same scene in the late afternoon and make a note of the colors that you see. Find matching colors in fabric and do a rough fabric paste-up of the "Landscape" using them.

If you like, do other variations of these exercises. It's always beneficial to stretch your color sensibilities and open yourself up to new color combinations. I hope these exercises make you more attuned to color: How it is affected by light and the time of day, how one color affects another, how color can have a profound effect on us, how even unappealing colors can be worked into an image.

"Color is all. When color is right, form is right. Color is everything, color is vibration like music; everything is vibration."
MARC CHAGALL

Use this line drawing of "Landscape" for the color exercises above.

"It will be useful too if he quit work often and take some relaxation; judgment will be clearer upon his return."
LEONARDO DA VINCI

STEP 2
MAKING A ROUGH FABRIC PASTE-UP

The next step is to make a rough fabric paste-up, a smaller version of the completed fabric artwork with the final selection of fabrics in position. To make one, tape your pattern onto the worktable. Next to it tape a 50 percent reduction copy of the pattern that you photocopied or designed at the end of Chapter 2. Have the other reduced copy nearby as a guide, because the fabrics used in your rough fabric paste-up may cover up most of your pattern and you don't want to miss any of the shapes.

With all of your fabric choices sorted into piles on your worktable and a reduced pattern as your guide, try out different combinations of fabrics by positioning your fabrics on top of the full-size pattern. Keep experimenting, folding your fabrics to create the approximate size of the shapes in your pattern or, in some cases, roughly cutting out the smaller shapes and adding them to the rough fabric paste-up. Make decisions about what works best for the final look that you envision.

When you are satisfied with your choices, cut out smaller versions of the shapes from the fabrics that you've chosen and glue or tape the pieces in place onto the reduced copy of your pattern taped to your worktable. The taped-down collage, made up of pieces of fabric, is your rough fabric paste-up (see photo below left). It will be your guide for the next step.

This is another moment when it's a good idea to step away from your work for a snack or a walk around the block. When you return and look at the rough fabric paste-up with fresh eyes, you may decide to make some changes. (Sometimes it helps to squint your eyes to help visualize the final image.) Make any changes that are necessary. When you are satisfied with your fabric choices, then proceed.

Your worktable is still piled high with all of the fabrics that you had originally considered for this project. Save the larger pieces of the fabrics from which you cut the pieces used in the rough fabric paste-up and remove all the other fabrics from your worktable.

If the finished fabric artwork needs to be washable, you should pre-wash and dry your selected fabrics. If not, proceed to Step 3.

Once you've made your selection, assemble the chosen fabrics on your worktable.

Create a small rough fabric paste-up on the reduced copy of the pattern to show the final fabric choices.

STEP 3
PREPARING YOUR FABRIC

Based on the size of the shapes in your pattern, cut out generous pieces from your selected fabrics (see first photo at right). Keep the *pattern* and the *grain* of the fabric in mind and cut out your pieces accordingly. See the examples in the photo above right on page 45. For example, with striped or patterned fabric, make sure that you cut out enough fabric so that the stripes go in the correct direction when you cut out your shape. The grain is the direction of the fabric's fibers. Because the grain can change the color of a fabric if it is turned upside down or sideways, it's best to mark the top of your fabric with a dot or a piece of tape. In that way, you will know how to position your fabric on top of the pattern so that the fabric shapes will be consistent in terms of the grain.

When you come to the shapes that will be at the outer edges of the pattern, allow an extra $1^1/2$" of fabric at the outer edges beyond the size of your pattern. In this way, if you decide to turn your fabric artwork into a pillow, hanging, or artwork mounted on canvas stretchers or foam core, you will have enough fabric to hem or mount your stitched artwork. Set your iron on "cotton" and press the fabric pieces you've cut out, using spray starch and ironing the fabric on the back (see second photo). Next, iron paper-backed fusible webbing onto the backs of your fabric pieces, ironing just the center of each piece. Take care not to iron the fusible webbing onto your ironing board surface (see third photo). (See "How to Use Paper-Backed Fusible Webbing," below.)

Let your fused fabric cool. Then cut off any excess fusible webbing that is not attached to the fabric (see fourth photo). Iron the rest of the fabric pieces.

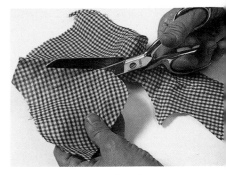

Cut out a generous piece from each fabric to allow room to position the pattern's shape in whatever way works best.

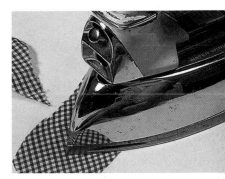

Iron all of your chosen fabrics.

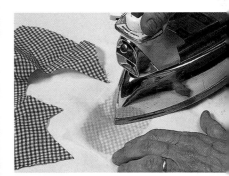

Using the tip of your iron, attach the fusible webbing to the back of your fabric by ironing a small area in the center of the paper backing (see box for details).

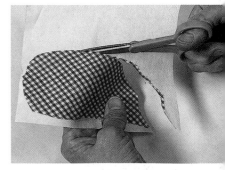

Cut off excess fusible webbing not attached to the fabric.

> **HINT**
> It's always wise to press your fabrics on the back. If you iron the front, the fabric's finish might be adversely affected by the iron and/or the spray starch.

HOW TO USE PAPER-BACKED FUSIBLE WEBBING

Step 1 Cut out a generous piece of fabric (larger than the shape that you intend to cut from the fabric). Then spray-starch the fabric and iron it.

Step 2 Put an 18"-x-24" piece of flat cardboard on your ironing board. Use smooth mat board or chipboard, not corrugated cardboard. Cut out a piece of paper-backed fusible webbing that is larger than the ironed fabric. Position the fabric on the cardboard *right side down*. Lay the fusible webbing on top of the fabric with the paper-backing side up. With your iron setting on "cotton," use the pointed tip of your iron to lightly iron a 2"-x-2" area in the center of the paper backing. The heat will fuse the fabric and webbing together in that area.

Step 3 Cut off any excess fusible webbing that extends beyond the edges of the fabric. If you wish, cut the fabric and webbing together, making a uniform edge as you cut. By doing this, you will avoid ironing the excess webbing onto your ironing board because the fusible webbing will, at this point, no longer extend beyond the fabric.

Step 4 Adhere the fusible webbing to the entire piece of fabric by ironing on the paper-backed side of your fabric. Rather than glide your iron, pick it up and put it down in the next position. Each time, count to five before picking up the iron and moving it to the next position. If you are working with a large piece of fabric, place the iron down in the center and work your way out to the edges. Since fabrics vary, experiment with scrap pieces to determine the right timing for the fusing process.

Step 5 Let the fused fabric cool before continuing.

With the aid of the light box, trace the lines onto the back of each piece of fabric or onto the paper backing of the fusible webbing (see Step 4).

The shape that in real life would be in front of another shape will overlap that shape in the project.

STEP 4
TRACING THE SHAPES AND DETERMINING UNDERLAP AND OVERLAP

This step is the tricky part: While the lines on your pattern will act as a guide, you will not necessarily trace the exact lines onto your fabric shapes. Think of creating fabric shapes like a jigsaw puzzle but with a slight underlap (see photo below left).

Before tracing your pattern onto the paper backing of your fabric pieces, visualize the shapes on your pattern as if they existed in real space. For example, in "Down on the Farm" the man with the guitar (sitting on the stairs) is in front of the stairs, and the stairs are in front of the house, and the house is in front of the grass, and the grass is in front of the mountains in the background, and the mountains are in front of the sky. So, add a $1/8$" underlap to each shape that is *visually behind* another shape. If it helps make things clearer, draw dotted lines on your pattern to indicate the $1/8$" underlap. Based on your pattern, you have to figure out which shape underlaps another shape. Begin with the shape that is visually "closest" to you and end with the shape that is "farthest away." The diagram below will help explain this concept.

- Shape A is in front of Shape B. Shape B includes a $1/8$" underlap in the center where Shape A overlaps it.
- Shape B is in front of Shape C. Shape C includes a $1/8$" underlap in the center where Shape B overlaps it.
- Shape C is in front of Shape D. Shape D includes a $1/8$" underlap in the center where Shape C overlaps it.
- Shape D will also include $1 1/2$" of extra fabric on all of the outside edges so that the finished fabric artwork can be stretched on canvas stretchers, made into a pillow, or framed as a hanging.

HINT
Put a dot at the top of the back of each shape. This will help you orient your shapes later in Step 9. It is also helpful to number the shapes on the paper backing corresponding to matching numbers that you write on your pattern.

This simplified pattern will show you how to cut the shapes and how they overlap each other when they are assembled.

PATTERN

SHAPE A
Shape A is the same size as shown on the pattern.

SHAPE B
The outside edge of Shape B is the same as shown on the pattern. For the inside edge of Shape B, add extra for underlapping Shape A.

SHAPE C
The outside edge of Shape C is the same as on the pattern. For the inside edge of Shape C, add extra for underlapping Shape B.

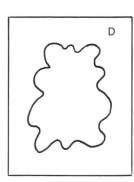

SHAPE D
On all outside edges of Shape D, add extra in case you want to stretch the finished art on canvas stretchers or make it into a pillow. On Shape D's inside edge, add extra for underlapping Shape C.

Turn your pattern over and tape it onto the light box *right side down.* Start with the shape on your pattern that is closest to the foreground. Consult your rough fabric paste-up to determine which fabric will be used for that shape. (If the fabric has stripes, a printed pattern, or a specific grain, take care to orient the fabric so that it will be positioned correctly in the finished artwork.) (See photo at right.)

Place your fabric *wrong side up* on top of the pattern. Keeping the 1/8" underlap concept in mind, use a Pentel marker to trace the shape onto the paper backing of the prepared fabric (see photo above left on facing page). (Or peel off the paper backing and, using a Stabilo pencil, trace the shape right onto the back of the fabric.)

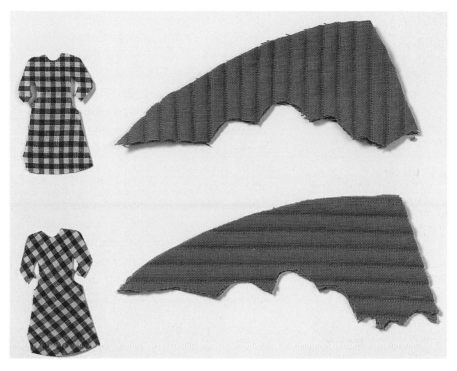

Make sure that the fabric is correctly positioned in relation to the shape and how you want the shape to appear in the finished project

> **HINT**
>
> Do not use a ballpoint pen to draw your lines. It might smudge onto your fabric.

WHY INCLUDE A 1/8" UNDERLAP?

Without a 1/8" underlap, each shape would "butt up" against the adjacent shapes like a real jigsaw puzzle and you would have to stitch down *all* the edges of *all* the shapes. By including an underlap where the two shapes meet, you only have to stitch down one edge rather than two. Besides eliminating unnecessary stitching, creating an underlap simplifies your image and makes the composition more concise. It also adds to the illusion that your shapes exist in three-dimensional reality. (When you sew down the shapes in Step 11, your zigzag stitching will cover over the slightly raised edge caused by the underlap.) By creating precise 1/8" underlaps, you will eliminate unnecessary lumps under your shapes. (To see what I mean, look at the photo at right as an example of what not to do. Notice the awkward lump in the frying pan made by the rounded edge of the container.)

> **HINT**
>
> In the finished artwork, fabric shapes that underlap other shapes may cause awkward lumps and bumps. Be sure to eliminate everything under your shapes that is not necessary, *leaving just a 1/8" underlap.*

In "*CUE* Magazine Still Life," 14" x 11" (1973), note where the shape of the canister created a lump under the frying pan shape. Try to avoid this.
Originally appeared as a *CUE* Magazine cover, 1973.

If it is difficult to see through the fabric, peel off the paper backing of the fusible webbing and, using a Pentel marker or a Pigma Micron pen, trace the shape onto the back of the paper backing. Then reposition the paper backing onto the back of the fabric and re-iron it in place. Set all the traced fabric shapes aside to be cut later in Step 8.

Next, consult your rough fabric paste-up. Use the fabric for the shape that visually underlaps your first shape and trace the shape onto the paper backing of the fusible webbing, adding an additional 1/8" of fabric where it visually underlaps the first shape.

Continue in the same way with the other shapes. When you come to the shapes located at the outside edges of the pattern, add an extra 1 1/2" to all the outside edges. This will give you enough extra fabric to stretch the finished artwork onto canvas stretchers, or make it into a quilted hanging or a pillow. Once you have traced all the shapes, set them aside to be cut later in Step 8.

STEP 5
BACKING FABRIC

Cut out a piece of white cotton duck fabric 1 1/2" larger on all sides than the size of your pattern (see photos at left). Remember to orient the direction of your fabric correctly. Iron the backing fabric using spray starch. All of your shapes will be positioned on top of this backing fabric.

STEP 6
PADDED OPTIONS:
SELECTIVE AND OVERALL
PADDING

I didn't use any padding in "Down on the Farm" but you might want this effect in this image and/or in other projects. Following is information about selective padding (adding dimension only to certain areas of your artwork) and overall padding (creating a quilted, overall padded surface for the entire artwork).

Selective Padding To add dimension to certain shapes in your artwork, cut out a piece of white felt that is 3/8" smaller than the shapes you want to pad. In Step 9 you will position these felt shapes under the fabric shapes. (More information and photographs of this technique are given in Chapter 6, "Using Selective Padding," which begins on page 77.)

To get a straight line for the backing fabric, pull a thread on all sides (see Step 5).

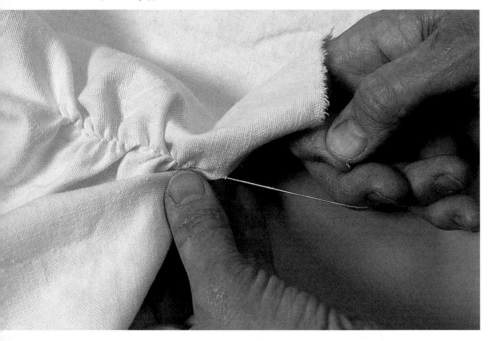

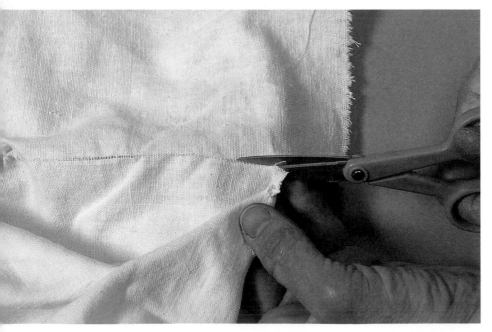

Cut along the channel in the backing fabric.

Overall Padding For an overall quilted effect for your finished artwork, cut out a piece of lightweight white batiste fabric (backed with fusible webbing) that is 1¹/₂" larger on all sides than the size of your pattern. In Step 9 you will position your shapes onto the batiste fabric and then layer the batting between the batiste fabric and the backing fabric. (This technique is explained in Chapter 7, "Using Overall Padding," which begins on page 85.)

bers you used for the corresponding padding shapes so that you will be able to determine which padding shape relates to which fabric shape.

Remove the paper backing from the backs of the fabric shapes. Lightly spray the backs of all the shapes with spray adhesive (see photo below right).

Cut out each shape carefully (see Step 8).

STEP 7
PREPARING A STICKY BOARD

A sticky board is used to hold your fabric shapes in place when you spray them with a light coating of spray adhesive in Step 8. (Without a sticky surface on the cardboard, your fabric shapes may get scattered by the pressurized air from the spray adhesive.)

To make a sticky board, lightly spray one side of a piece of 18"-x-24" cardboard with spray adhesive.

STEP 8
CUTTING OUT THE FABRIC SHAPES

Using sharp scissors, carefully cut out all of the fabric shapes (see photo above right). Then lightly position the shapes *right side down* on the spray-glued surface of the sticky board.

Position the fabric shapes on the sticky board with the tops of the shapes pointing toward the top of the board. Arrange them in the same relationship as they will appear in your fabric artwork. This will help you recognize the shapes as you position them onto the backing fabric in Step 9.

If you had decided on the *selective padding* option in Step 6, position your padded shapes on the cardboard *right side down* next to the fabric shapes that will overlap them in Step 9. Number your fabric shapes with the same num-

Spray the backs of all of the fabric shapes with a light coating of spray adhesive (see Step 8).

Step 9
Putting It All Together

Tape your pattern onto the light box, this time with the *right side up*. Tape your backing fabric on top of the pattern. You might be tempted to trace your pattern directly onto the backing fabric, but this is *not* advisable because those lines may show through your fabric shapes and be visible in your finished artwork. Position the fabric shapes in place, starting with the background shapes and working your way to the shapes that are visually in the foreground (see photo above left). If you have difficulty seeing the pattern through the backing fabric, tape an additional transparent pattern *right side up* on top of the backing fabric (lining it up with the pattern that is underneath the backing fabric).

NOTE If you chose the *selective padding* effect in Step 6, position each padding shape underneath the corresponding fabric shape on the backing fabric. If you decided on the *overall padding* effect in Step 6, position your fabric shapes on a piece of white batiste fabric that is 1^1/2" larger on all sides than your pattern.

This is the time to look at the assembled artwork and make any necessary adjustments. Make sure that your overlaps are correct and that your fabrics' pattern, grain, and orientation are all correct. At this point you may decide to substitute a different fabric or add some additional shapes to your artwork.

When you have made any necessary adjustments, remove the tape from the backing fabric. Slide a clean piece of cardboard underneath your artwork, being careful to keep all the shapes in place. Bring it all over to your ironing board.

Step 10
Ironing the Artwork

Set your iron on "cotton." Cover the shapes with a pressing cloth (see photo below left). Fuse down all of the shapes by ironing them onto the backing (or batiste) fabric.

NOTE For the *overall padding* effect: Iron the shapes in place onto the light-

"A picture is not thought out and settled beforehand. While it is being done it changes as one's thoughts change."
PABLO PICASSO

Position the shapes, using tweezers if necessary (see Step 9).

Use a pressing cloth when fusing all of the shapes in place with your iron (see Step 10).

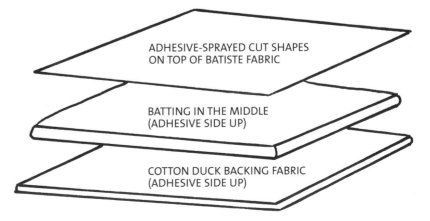

ADHESIVE-SPRAYED CUT SHAPES
ON TOP OF BATISTE FABRIC

BATTING IN THE MIDDLE
(ADHESIVE SIDE UP)

COTTON DUCK BACKING FABRIC
(ADHESIVE SIDE UP)

This is how all the layers of the overall padding effect look (see Step 10).

weight batiste fabric. Lightly spray adhesive on top of the cotton duck backing fabric and position a layer of lightweight batting (cut slightly smaller than the backing fabric) on top of the adhesive-sprayed backing fabric. Then lightly spray adhesive on top of the batting. Position the batiste fabric *right side up* on top of the adhesive-sprayed batting. Using a pressing cloth and iron set on "cotton," iron it all in place. You will now have a sandwich of the two white fabrics with the batting inside (see diagram on facing page). To make sure that everything stays in place, use some long straight pins or baste around the edges.

STEP 11
SEWING THE ARTWORK

Choose threads that match the colors of all the fabrics that you have used in your artwork. Start by sewing a loose zigzag sewing-machine stitch around the outer perimeter of the entire artwork. Then, use thread that matches the color of each shape to sew down all of the edges of your shapes with a moderately tight zigzag stitch (see photo above right). The stitch should not straddle the cut edge of the fabric shapes. Rather it should cover the edge and extend $1/16"$ to $1/8"$ onto the shape that you are stitching down (see diagram at right).

STEP 12
FINAL DETAILS

When the zigzag stitching is completed, you may add embellishments, decorative stitching, or hand embroidery. When you are finished, you may staple your artwork onto a piece of foam core or canvas stretchers (see photo below right). You may then decide to frame it. Or, instead of stapling it down, you could make it into a pillow or a hanging. Chapter 4, which begins on page 57, provides instructions for additional ways to use your completed artwork.

Stitch the shapes into place with a zigzag sewing-machine stitch (see Step 11).

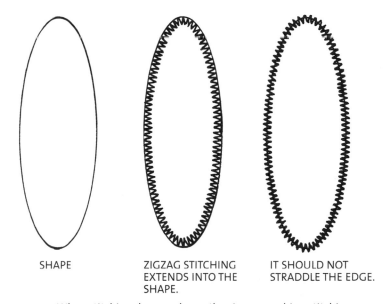

SHAPE · ZIGZAG STITCHING EXTENDS INTO THE SHAPE. · IT SHOULD NOT STRADDLE THE EDGE.

When stitching down a shape, the zigzag machine stitching extends into the shape but does not straddle the edge of the shape (see Step 11).

Once the stitching is completed, the artwork is stapled onto canvas stretchers (see Step 12).

Framing Stitched Artwork by Rick Gottas

Framing Artwork That Is Stapled onto Canvas Stretchers

If the artwork has been stapled onto stretcher bars (canvas stretchers), the biggest issue in selecting the frame will be the depth of the molding itself. The molding will need to be at least as deep as the stretcher bar is thick, in order for the stretcher bars to be completely covered from the side view. Anything less will leave a portion of the stretcher bar visible when the frame is hung on the wall. For this reason it is a good idea to select the thinnest stretcher bar material possible before stretching your work over it. Stretcher bars usually are available in junior, regular, and jumbo sizes.

There are essentially two choices in designing the framing for work on stretchers. Either you will frame it "up close" with a frame directly surrounding the piece, or you can frame it using a liner and an outer frame. (A liner is a molding covered with fabric.) The liner will give the artwork a look similar to that of a matted piece. Liners come in a wide variety of widths, shapes, and depths and are pre-covered in neutral fabrics. Your framer may also offer you a selection of linens, silks, suedes, or other fabrics to choose from. You may also be able to use your own fabric.

If you use a liner, you will need an even deeper outside molding, because you now will need to hide the stretcher and the covered liner. As a general rule, a wider frame will give your finished artwork more presence on the wall and protect it from looking as if it is being swallowed by the wall.

When choosing your frame, try not to use any color that you want to "bring out" in the finished piece. If you do you will produce the opposite effect: Adding more of the color will actually push the color into the background. At the very least, the finished artwork should be glazed with regular glass in order to protect it from airborne dirt, insects, and other hazards. However, the glass should not come in direct contact with the work. Ideally, your framer should incorporate the use of clear Lucite spacer bars that allow 3/16" of air space between the glass and the artwork. When the glazing is placed on top of a liner, the glass protects the liner and the artwork and the liner acts as the spacer between the art and the glass.

The stretcher bar can be secured to the frame with glazing points or with offset clips. To further protect the artwork from dust and insects, the back of the frame should be sealed with a dust cover, at the very least. For better protection, an archival board can be stapled or glued to the back of the frame and the edges taped all the way around.

Framing Artwork That Has Been Stretched on Foam Core

Artwork that has been stretched over foam core can be framed either with or without a liner or a mat.

If you are using a mat, it is recommended that the mat either be a double thick (8 ply) or a double mat (two mats that are 4 ply each), in order to keep the glazing from touching the artwork.

If you are using a simple frame used "up close" (without a border or a mat), the artwork can be secured into the frame by placing an acid-free foam core board behind the frame and then securing it to the frame with a point driver.

If you are using a mat, cut the mat opening and then cut an identical-size piece of mat or foam core board. Place the artwork on the backing board and line up the mat over the artwork. Fill in the gaps between the edges of the artwork and the outer dimension of the mat with strips of acid-free foam core so that the artwork is held firmly in position.

Alternatively, you may want your framer to cut a sink mat the exact same size as the foam core over which you have stretched your artwork. You should then be able to place a piece of glazing on top of the matted and backed artwork and place this package into your frame. The artwork can be secured with glazing points and then sealed by taping the edges of the frame and glazing points.

Again, when choosing mats it is a good idea to refrain from using any color that you want to "bring out" in the finished piece. If you do, you will produce the opposite effect: Adding more of the color will actually push it into the background.

When using double mats, a darker mat on the inside creates a shadow effect and adds depth to the composition. Try varying the width of the inner mat from 1/8" to 1" until the effect is just right.

Framing Free-Hanging Artwork (perhaps in a shadow box)

If you have a piece of stitched artwork that you would like to "float" in order to show all of the edges, you will need to have your framer strategically stitch it to a museum-quality 4 ply archival mount board, at least 8 ply board for heavier pieces. A fabric-covered board would probably be a better choice than a plain paper mat board. Again, your framer may offer many selections to choose from or you may supply your own fabrics. You may choose to float your artwork on a simple backing as described, or you may want to float it inside a deep mat before placing it in the frame.

Framing Free-Hanging Artwork 18" x 24" or Larger

Occasionally fabric-based art is large enough and heavy enough to consider the use of hanging sleeves and dowels at the top and bottom of the artwork. The bottom sleeve is useful in keeping the artwork flat at the bottom dimension. Many works have a tendency to curl, either because of their construction or due to changes in temperature and humidity over time.

The top sleeves should be a bit shorter than the total width of the piece so that the dowels or lathe are visible at the back. A small hole can be drilled into the rod or lathe so that the piece can be sewn to the backing board and into the appropriate position. It is a good idea to seal any wooden dowels or lathe with a clear lacquer or stain-killing primer in order to protect the piece from discoloration over time. Wood products will leach acids onto the cloth and will stain it. (Some artists choose aluminum lathe or dowels instead of wood for this reason.) After placing the dowel in the bottom sleeve, both ends of the sleeve can be sewn shut.

The dowels are usually attached to the backing only at the top, allowing the bottom to hang freely. A spacer deep enough to keep the glazing from coming into contact with the pieces will need to be placed inside the frame. For a clean effect, it can be covered with the same material used as your background.

USING ACID-FREE MATERIALS

Ask your framer to use acid-free mat boards, museum boards, or acid-free foam boards in all aspects of the framing project. These materials are designed to protect your work from acid burns and staining that are transferred to your artwork over time when inferior products such as regular mat board and regular corrugated cardboard are used in the frame.

To protect your artwork from the ravages of light, use glass that filters out 99 percent of the ultraviolet light. There are a variety of choices and price points for each of these products. Museum glass eliminates 99 percent of the UV rays and also reduces reflection by about 95 percent, giving you brighter color and the look of no glass.

USING GLASS OR PLEXIGLAS

For the ultimate in safety and protection for your most valuable and cherished works, use Plexiglas that eliminates 99 percent of the UV rays. This product has the added advantage of being virtually unbreakable. Should your artwork fall, be hit by an errant baseball, or whatever, it will be protected from the potential damage associated with broken shards of glass. When framing larger works, Plexiglas also will reduce the overall weight of the framed piece.

"Nostalgic Portrait" was backed with fabric, then a piece of foam core was inserted and the artwork and backing fabric were stitched together. The artwork was attached to a mat board and framed with a decorative wooden frame and glass.

ADVICE ON LIGHTING

When lighting your artwork, try to use halogen bulbs. Halogen bulbs will enhance your work with clear and true color. Regular incandescent lightbulbs add reds to your work and change the normal color relationships. If your artwork has been glazed with UV-filtering glass, there is no need to worry about fading under halogen light.

CARING FOR AND/OR STORING UNFRAMED ARTWORK

When storing unframed artwork, make sure that it is lightly wrapped and placed in an archival box in an environment that is temperature controlled and dry. Archival boxes can be made of acid-free foam core or archival mat boards or purchased at photography and better art supply stores.

RICK GOTTAS has been designing and fabricating frames since 1975 as the owner/director of The American Art Company, an upscale gallery also offering custom framing services in Tacoma, Washington. The gallery actively represents the work of Erika Carter and Rachel Brumer, Nancy Erickson, Donna Prichard, and Janet Steadman. Also, since 1989 Rick Gottas has produced and curated seven Northwest Quilt Invitationals, which feature as many as twenty-seven artists and forty quilts in each exhibition. He is currently a board member of Studio Art Quilt Associates.

The Creative Process

Having explored how to develop your pattern in Chapter 2 and completed your project in Chapter 3, it's fitting that this Creative Process gallery is next. It will give you a "behind-the-scenes" look at how images evolve from the rough beginnings of a thumbnail sketch, through the pattern development and fabric paste-up, to the completed artwork. The earliest image in this gallery is "Yankee Still Life" (shown on the facing page) and the most recent is "Town and Country" (shown below).

TOWN AND COUNTRY

The story this artwork illustrates has a simple "country mouse/city mouse" theme—some people enjoy country life; others prefer to live in the city. Like most of my appliquéd illustration projects, this commission had a very short deadline—about a week.

*"Come. Quickly. You mustn't miss the dawn.
It will never be just like this again."*
GEORGIA O'KEEFFE

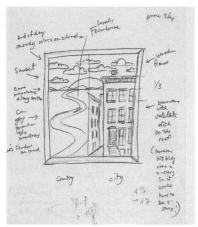
Rough Sketch

Drawing

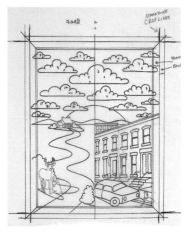
Pattern

Rough Fabric Paste-up

Town and Country
13¹/₂" x 10" (2004)
Commissioned by *The Washington Post* for magazine cover. Collection of Karen Hollinger.

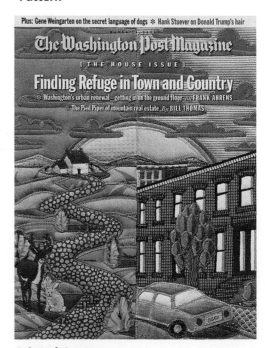
Printed Cover

YANKEE STILL LIFE

I set up and photographed several still lifes, using a variety of foods and an assortment of dishes. To create an element of realism, I dyed the top of the pale asparagus fabric a darker shade of green and air-brushed parts of the lace background plus the tomato and pepper fabrics with brown paint to create the illusion of volume.

Photo of Actual Still Life

Rough Fabric Paste-Up

Pattern

Yankee Still Life
16" x 20" (1983)
Yankee Magazine.
Collection of Jack Miller.

FULTON STREET MALL

This was one of the most intense projects I've ever taken on. To draw the buildings, I needed to photograph them straight on (not from street level). To do this I used a "cherry picker"—and was hoisted up more than twenty feet in the air.

Fulton Street Mall
15" x 72" (1986)
Commissioned by Fulton Mall Association for bus poster

Original Sketch and Reference Photos

Sketch of a Store

Poster on the Bus

CAUSE AND EFFECT

This image comes with an emotional history. Both portraits are of my brother, James Weaver. On the left, he's shown at twenty-eight years old, in the year that unfortunately he was in a motorcycle accident and died. In 2000, when I created "Cause and Effect," I realized that even though James was my older brother, I had survived him by more years than he had lived.

Black-and-White Photo

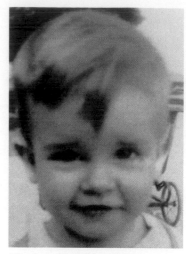
Black-and-White Photo

Value Study

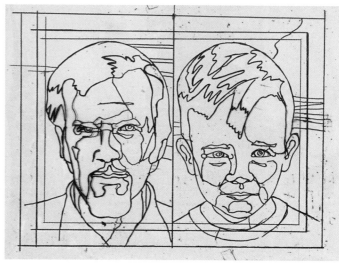
Pattern

Rough Fabric Paste-up

Cause and Effect
8" x 10" x 1" (2000)

SELF-PORTRAIT IN CHECKERBOARD

I created this artwork as an ode to Andy Warhol's technique of using four quadrants of the same image with color variations. It was exhilarating to be totally unconcerned that my face was lavender in one square and bright yellow in the next—a fun experiment in color.

Original Photo and Enlargement

Value Study

Pattern

Polaroid Photo of Rough Fabric Paste-up

Fabric Choices

Self-Portrait in Checkerboard
19³/4" x 15¹/2" (1996)

CHAPTER 4

Many Uses for the Same Artwork

I have always loved symmetry, the work of William Morris, and folk art images of flowers. "Floral Border" embraces all of these interests. It also harkens back to frakturs, which are a type of nineteenth-century Pennsylvania Dutch document. Frakturs were highly embellished marriage or birth certificates, hand-made with pen, ink, and watercolor.

Design motifs such as those on frakturs were usually symmetrical. The motifs were used on quilts, cut-work paper valentines, furniture, plates, and even tombstones. These hand-decorated objects were cherished as family heirlooms. Perhaps your "Floral Border" artwork will be cherished by your descendants.

This chapter will explain how to create a decorative stitched border, and then use it as a pillow, picture frame, scrapbook cover, and greeting card. I hope you also will apply these techniques to the artwork shown in the other chapters.

Floral Border
18" x 16" (2004)

Stitching "Floral Border"

MATERIALS NEEDED
🌹

NOTE The quantity and size of the materials will depend on the size in which you choose to work. In addition to the materials in the General Materials Needed lists on pages 30 and 40, you will need the following:

stiff cardboard
(for the picture frame on page 60)

felt
(for the picture frame on page 60 and the scrapbook cover on page 62)

pillow stuffing
(for the pillows on pages 59 and 63)

paper-backed fabric prints
(for the scrapbook cover on page 62 and the pillows on pages 59 and 63)

X-Acto knife
(for the greeting card on page 63)

X-Acto knife or band saw
(for the picture frame on page 60)

Bristol plate white paper
(for the greeting card on page 63)

Gudy paper-backed adhesive
(for the greeting card on page 63)

emery board or sandpaper
(for the picture frame on page 60)

🌹

To create "Floral Border" enlarge the "Floral Border" Picture Frame pattern that appears on page 115.

Follow Steps 1 to 11 on pages 40 to 49, and then follow the instructions on the following pages that are specific to the project you would like to create.

I've included a variety of color combinations for "Floral Border" (see photos at right). Each gives this project a different "personality." Choose one of these or experiment with other color combinations of your own. (For more information on color, see page 41.)

On the following pages, you will learn how "Floral Border" can be used in several different ways. You can:

- make "Floral Border" into a stitched pillow
- stitch a special picture frame for a favorite photograph
- photograph or scan the finished artwork and then print it onto fabric. (Also, by scanning the artwork on a computer, the individual colors can be manipulated to create a wide variety of color combinations.) Then you can use the printed fabric copies to make a pillow, scrapbook cover, or picture frame.
- print smaller copies of the stitched "Floral Border" onto paper and make the paper prints into greeting cards.

These rough fabric paste-ups show several color schemes for "Floral Border."

I have cut out the fabric shapes and fused them in place.

HINT

In Step 4, put a small piece of white tape in the center of the front side of each of the four outside edges of your background fabric. Draw a line on the tape at the midpoint of each of the four sides. Without marking directly on the fabric, this will help you position your artwork correctly in any of the options shown here.

Stitched-Fabric Projects

STITCHED-FABRIC PILLOW

To make your stitched artwork into a pillow, enlarge the "Floral Border" Pillow pattern that appears on page 115. Then follow Steps 1 to 11 on pages 40 to 49.

After Step 11, cut out a piece of fabric that is the same size as the background fabric of your stitched artwork. (It could be the same color as your background fabric or a color that complements it.) Put the fabric on top of your stitched artwork *right side to right side*. Pin the two pieces together at the edges with the pins pointing toward the fabrics' outer edges.

Machine-sew a running stitch $1/2$" inside the outer edges around the entire project. Leave a 5" opening at the center of the bottom of the pillow. At the corners of the pillow, trim off some of the fabric at an angle (see diagram below left).

Turn the pillow right side out. Use a blunt knitting needle to gently push out the corners of the pillow. Then stuff the pillow with pillow stuffing (see photo below right). Either sew a zipper at the opening or hand-sew the pillow closed with a blind stitch.

This photo shows a completed $9^1/2$"-x-$7^1/2$" "Floral Border" pillow. It was made from a fabric print (see pages 62 to 63). You can also make a pillow from the original stitched "Floral Border."

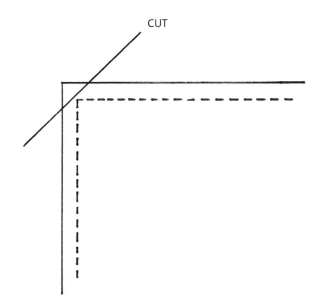

This diagram shows where to cut off the fabric at the corners.

The pillow is stuffed with polyester batting.

STITCHED-FABRIC PICTURE FRAME

To make "Floral Border" as a frame for a photograph, iron fusible webbing onto the back of the stitched artwork. Remove the paper backing. Enlarge the patterns for Cardboard A and Cardboard B that appear on page 116 to the size that will accommodate your photograph. For example, if you are making a frame that is 12³/4" high and 10" wide with room for a photograph approximately 6" x 4", cut out two 12³/4"-x-10" pieces of sturdy cardboard: Cardboards A and B (see photos below).

Enlarge the "Floral Border" Picture Frame pattern that appears on page 117 and trace the oval shape onto Cardboard A. Use the X-Acto knife (or, if the card-

board is very thick, use a band saw) to cut out the oval shape. (This oval will be the space for your photograph in the finished frame.) Sand the cut edges of the oval with an emery board or sandpaper. Mark the midpoint of all four outside edges of Cardboards A and B on both the front and the back. Trace the oval from Cardboard A onto the front of Cardboard B.

Using paint that matches the color of your artwork's background fabric, on Cardboard B, paint the top edge plus 1" down on both the front and back. Also paint a 1" triangle on both the front and back at the four corners of both cardboards (see bottom photo below). On Cardboard A, paint the inside edges of the cut oval. Also paint the ¹/4" extending beyond the oval on both sides of Cardboard A. Set both pieces of cardboard aside. (Painting these edges will help when the stitched artwork is attached to Cardboards A and B.)

To pad your stitched frame, cut out a piece of white felt that matches the shape of Cardboard A. Spray adhesive on the back of the felt and position it onto the front of Cardboard A.

Tape the pattern to the light box and position Cardboard A *front side up* on top of the pattern. Line up the midpoints on the pattern and Cardboard A. Remove the paper backing of your stitched artwork and lightly spray adhesive on its back. Position it on top of the felt padding on Cardboard A. Again, make sure that the midpoints are lined up. With a colored pencil that matches the color of your background fabric, trace Cardboard A's oval onto the front of your stitched artwork. This is Line 1 (see photo above on facing page).

With a Stabilo pencil that contrasts with the color of your background fabric, draw an oval shape onto the front of the artwork ³/4" inside Line 1's oval. This is Line 2 (see photo above on facing page). Cut on Line 2 and remove this fabric.

This is the front of Cardboards A (left) and B (right). On Cardboard A, the fabric tab on the top has been fused to the back. On Cardboard B, the felt has been glued down.

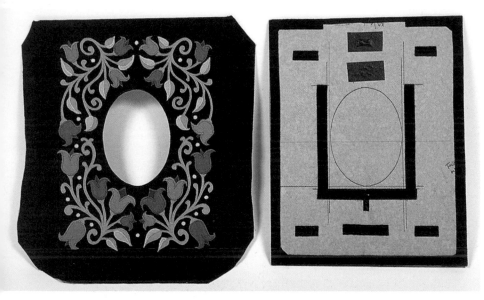

This is the back of Cardboards A and B. Notice the top tab fused in place on the back of Cardboard A and the ring and flap stitched to the back of Cardboard B.

With small, sharp scissors, carefully cut out V shapes toward Line 2, thereby creating fabric tabs (see photo at right).

Fold the tabs to the back of Cardboard A. Use white artist's tape to temporarily hold the tabs in place. Turn the artwork over. Cover the front of the artwork with a pressing cloth. Set your iron on "cotton" and fuse "Floral Border" onto the felt by pressing it with the iron. After the artwork cools, turn it over and undo the taped tabs. Reposition them as needed. Set your iron on "cotton" and iron down the tabs to fuse them in place.

To cover any cut lines on the inside of the oval, glue a $1/8$" piece of ribbon to the inside of the oval shape. The ribbon may either match or complement the color of the background fabric.

Cut out pieces of $1/2$"-wide black felt. Glue them onto the front side of Cardboard B (see photo above right on facing page and Cardboard B pattern on page 116 for help in positioning). The felt will keep a consistent distance between Cardboards A and B, as well as provide a space for your photograph to rest once it slides through the opening at the top of your finished picture frame.

Turn over Cardboard A and trim off the excess fabric on all four sides, leaving $1^1/2$" of the fabric extending beyond the edges of Cardboard A. Fold over the top $1^1/2$" flap of fabric onto the back of Cardboard A and adhere it in place with white glue (see photo below left on facing

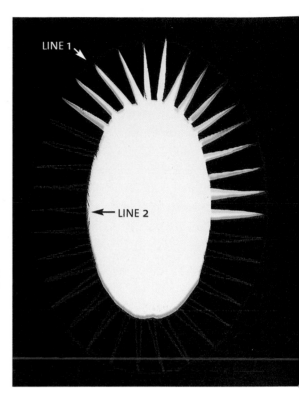

LINE 1

←—— LINE 2

Follow the directions to cut V-shaped tabs in the oval cutout area.

page). Use white artist's tape to temporarily hold it down. Let the glue dry and then remove the white tape.

If your frame is to hang on the wall, sew a small ring onto the back of Cardboard B (see photo below right on facing page). If it is to sit on a table, enlarge the pattern for Cardboard C that appears on page 117. Trace the pattern onto a piece of cardboard, cut out the cardboard, and paint it black. Poke holes in the top of Cardboard C and sew it onto the back of Cardboard B. Attach a ribbon to the backs of Cardboard B and C to hold Cardboard C in position. Then position Cardboard B (*with its painted edge on top*) behind Cardboard A. Glue the other three $1^1/2$" flaps of your artwork to the back of Cardboard B. Use white artist's tape to temporarily hold down the flaps. Use several heavy telephone books or other weights to press it down. Let the glue dry and then remove the white tape.

Cut out a piece of black felt $1/8$" smaller on all sides than Cardboard B. To position the felt onto the back of Cardboard B, you will have to cut into the felt so that it will fit over the ring and/or Cardboard C. Use white glue or Gudy paper-backed adhesive on the felt. If you use white glue, use several heavy telephone books or other weights to press it down until the glue dries and you are sure that the felt is firmly attached.

Slip your photograph into the opening at the top of your frame. If needed, add a thin piece of cardboard behind the photo so it fits snugly in place. (See the Hint for tips on positioning your photo.)

Here is the completed $12^3/4$"-x-10" "Floral Border" picture frame.

HINT

This will help you in positioning your photograph. Since there is a distance between the top of your picture frame and the oval opening, tape your photograph to the bottom of a piece of paper that matches the color of your background fabric and is a little longer than the distance from the top of your frame to the bottom of the oval and as wide as the width of the oval. Use this "extender" to drop your photo down the slot and position is correctly in place.

Printed-Fabric Projects

HINT

If your scrapbook is a different size than what is shown, add 3/16" to all sides of the Fabric pattern. This will account for the thickness of the scrapbook cover.

When your "Floral Border" artwork is completed, use a camera, scanner, and/or computer to scan and print onto paper-backed fabric in a range of sizes (see "Resources"). If you do not have these tools and/or expertise, purchase paper-backed fabric and have your local copier store scan and print your "Floral Border" artwork onto the fabric. After printing, remove the paper backing and use the fabric as you would any other piece of fabric.

PRINTED-FABRIC SCRAPBOOK COVER

To make a printed-fabric scrapbook cover 12^1/2" x 13^1/2", enlarge the "Floral Border" Scrapbook Cover—Fabric pattern that appears on page 118. Print two copies of your "Floral Border" artwork, each approximately 9^3/4" high. Cut one of the prints in half horizontally and position the top half above the matching part of the other print. Position the bottom half below the corresponding part of the other print (see photo below left). Pin them *right side to right side* and machine-sew the pieces together with a running stitch. Press the seams flat.

(*Optional*) To create a padded, trapunto effect, cut a piece of felt and a piece of lightweight batiste fabric, each 12^1/2" x 13^1/2". Sandwich the felt between the patched "Floral Border" printed fabric and the batiste fabric. Pin the layers together. Machine-sew a running stitch around the leaves, vines, and flowers to create a trapunto effect.

To complete the front of the scrapbook cover, cut a piece of fabric 13^7/8" x 28^5/8" that matches the color of the background fabric of the "Floral Border" printed fabric. Pin the two pieces of fabric *right side to right side* to the *left* of the patched "Floral Border" printed fabric. Machine-sew the pieces together. Press the seams flat.

Cut a piece of fabric 13^7/8" x 13^3/8" that matches the color of the background fabric of the "Floral Border" printed fabric. Pin the two pieces of fabric *right side to right side* to the *right* of the patched "Floral Border" printed fabric. Sew the pieces together. Press the seams flat. (NOTE You should have a piece of fabric that is 13^7/8" x 49^1/2". This is the front of your scrapbook cover.)

Iron paper-backed fusible webbing to the back of a piece of felt 15" x 50". Enlarge the "Floral Border" Scrapbook Cover—Felt Pieces pattern that appears on page 118 and use it to cut out the felt pieces.

Remove the paper backing and spray adhesive on the sides of the felt pieces that have the fusible webbing on them. Position the felt pieces on the back of the fabric you pieced together above. (Use the "Floral Border" Scrapbook Cover—Felt Pieces pattern as a guide.)

This 12^1/2"-x-13^1/2" scrapbook was made from two fabric prints of "Floral Border."

Set your iron on "cotton" and fuse the felt pieces in place.

Cut a piece of fabric 13$7/8$" x 49$1/2$" in the same color as the fabric you pieced together above. Position both fabrics *right side to right side*. Pin them together and machine-sew $1/4$" from the edge with a running stitch, leaving a 5" opening at the bottom. At each of the corners of the scrapbook cover, trim off some of the fabric at an angle (see diagram on page 59).

Turn the scrapbook cover *right side out* and use a blunt knitting needle to gently push out the corners. Position the "Floral Border" scrapbook cover over the scrapbook. Fold the front and back inside covers over and pin them in place. Pin the opening closed and blind-stitch it by hand. Blind-stitch the front cover to the inside front cover. Then blind-stitch the back cover to the inside back cover. Insert your scrapbook.

PRINTED-PAPER GREETING CARD

To make a paper greeting card, print a small copy of "Floral Border" onto paper (I used glossy photo paper). Enlarge the "Floral Border" Greeting Card pattern that appears on page 115. Position the print over the pattern. Trace the oval onto the print. Use an X-Acto knife to cut out the oval center so you can insert a photograph.

Cut out a piece of Bristol plate paper 7" x 10". Score and fold it in half to create a card that is 7" x 5". Tape the folded card to the light box. Place the paper print of "Floral Border" and center it on top of the front of the card. Mark and trim off any of the paper print that extends beyond the card.

After trimming, tape the paper print on top of the card. With a pencil, trace the shape of the oval cutout onto the front of the card. Then open the card and tape it to the light box. Center your photograph over the card's oval pencil line. With a Stabilo pencil, draw a line on the front of the photograph $1/4$"

beyond the edge of the card's pencil line. Trim the photograph on the line.

Use Gudy paper-backed adhesive to glue the photograph in place onto the front of the card (see "Using Paper-backed Adhesive"). Glue the paper print of "Floral Border" onto the front of the card using Gudy paper-backed adhesive.

PRINTED-FABRIC PILLOW

I created two pillows using printed fabric. (They are pictured on page 13.)

The smaller pillow was made with one 8$1/2$"-x-11" sheet of paper-backed fabric on which the "Floral Border" artwork was printed. To give it more dimension, I sandwiched a piece of felt between the fabric print and a piece of lightweight cotton. Then I machine-stitched around the outsides of the leaves, vines, and flowers to create a paper-backed padded, trapunto effect.

On the larger pillow I enlarged the image and made four separate fabric prints. (Each print included one-quarter of the whole image.) Then I carefully matched the four sections and sewed them together to form one rectangle. If you need help assembling the pillow, refer to the directions for "Stitched-Fabric Pillow" on page 59.

Here is a completed 7"-x-5" greeting card made from a paper print of "Floral Border."

HINT
Before you decide on the size of your greeting card, make sure you have an envelope of the correct size to fit it.

USING PAPER-BACKED ADHESIVE

Apply the sticky side of the paper-backed adhesive onto the back of your print. Burnish the back of the paper backing and then peel it off, leaving the adhesive in place. Position your photograph *glue side down* where you wish to adhere it. Cover your print with a piece of tracing paper and burnish it in place.

Fused Fabric and Dimensional

I hope you find these images intriguing. Perhaps the fused images shown on this page will tempt you to create fabric artwork using no stitching whatsoever. What I like most about this technique is that, because there's no stitching, there is absolutely nothing to separate the fabrics, nothing to keep each piece of fabric from influencing the fabric that's next to it. In this way, the patterns and colors of each fabric are intensified.

The dimensional images on the facing page were created for a variety of purposes and made from different materials. However, the fact that they are not flat—as most of my appliquéd images are—gives them a certain importance to me, even though creating them always presents more challenges than my appliquéd work.

On the Porch
7⁵/8" x 11¹/2" (1995)
Commissioned by Macmillan for *A Quilt Full of Memories* by Joanne Ryder. Courtesy of The McGraw-Hill Companies, Inc. Collection of Kathleen Ivans and Robert Bero.

Bill Clinton
14" x 11³/4" (1996)
From the estate of John Wylie Douglas

One Last Kiss
9" x 9" x 3" (1998)
Photo: D. James Dee

Ben Franklin
17" x 11" (2003)

Running in Time
9¹/2" x 5¹/2" (2003)
Commissioned by *The Wall Street Journal*

Agribusiness
15" x 18" x 15" (1981)
Commissioned by Deloitte & Touche USA LLP
for *Tempo* Magazine cover

Computer Art and Traditional Art in Bed with Each Other
30" x 24" x 3" (1999)
Originally appeared in the September/October 1999 issue of *PRINT*.

Money
8" x 12" (1990)

Grape costume
21" x 16" (2003)
From *Good Food* © 2004 by William H. Sadlier, Inc.
All rights reserved. Used with permission.

Some people think all we have to do is stick holes in the earth to find oil.

To pinpoint the oil and gas you need, we've got to do much more than that.

To begin with, there's the geophysical exploration and the leasing of the land. Last year, we paid over 500 million dollars for offshore leases alone—just for the right to *look* for oil and gas.

Still, we have to drill if we are to find out if there actually is oil or gas underground. Drilling can take up to a year or more. If oil or gas is discovered, we then can begin development drilling.

But drilling is risky and costly. Out of every 50 exploratory wells drilled in search of new oil or gas... only one on the average finds enough to be recovered in commercial amounts.

Then there's the cost. By the latest available figures, the average onshore well in 1973 cost $107,000, and offshore the average cost of a single well was $687,000. And if deep drilling is required, the well could cost as much as 1 million dollars or more.

And even if we find oil or gas,

our job isn't over. If a pipeline or storage system is needed, that's at least a two to six month job or even longer—at great cost. Then we have to get the oil to the refinery and manufacture it into the hundreds of products you need.

From the day we start looking for oil or gas to the day we can turn it into a finished product...it could take years and cost millions of dollars. The best way to supply you with the petroleum energy you need is through a free enterprise system that will enable us to generate the necessary capital.

TEXACO
We're working to keep your trust.

"Color possesses me. I don't have to pursue it. It will possess me always. I know it. This is the meaning of the happy. Color and I are one."
PAUL KLEE

Texaco Globe
5" x 6" x 6" (1975)
Reproduced with permission of Chevron U.S.A. Inc.

CHAPTER 5

Making a Banner

If your household is anything like ours, it seems as if friends and family members are always coming and going: leaving for business trips, coming back from college, or taking a vacation. With all this traveling, it's important to give those you love a colorful homecoming when they return. In this chapter, you'll learn how to create "Welcome Home" banner. Hang it indoors or out and show the world and your loved ones that you're glad they're back!

In order to make one that is generic at times but is also specific on other occasions, I've designed a banner that will provide a separate section for each family member or friend. In this way, you may add or substitute as many sections as you wish and even attach additional ones below one another. Also, you can create banners for other celebrations: birthdays, anniversaries, congratulations, and the like.

**"Welcome Home" basic banner,
with one section added**
29 1/2" x 16", plus 7" for name section

Getting Started

Materials Needed

In addition to the materials in the General Materials Needed lists on pages 30 and 40, you will need the following:

wooden dowels, 5/8" x 18"
(two for the basic "Welcome Home" banner, plus one for each personalized name section)

sandpaper

gesso

red acrylic paint

nylon canvas or ripstop nylon fabric, 1 yard of each of the colors
(used for the stripes, loops, and background fabric)

polyester twill iron-on polyester fabric, backed with heat-seal film, 1/2 yard
(used for the lettering)
(optional)

tacking iron

straight pins

cord or ribbon, approximately 24" to 30"

file folder

coated wire, approximately 18"
(1 1/2" for each S-shaped hook)

"Heat-and-Steam" fusible webbing
(optional)

tear-away paper

upholstery tacks

"Nothing can be rushed. It must grow, it should grow of itself."
PAUL KLEE

CHOOSING THE LETTERING

Experiment with different typefaces on your computer. Choose one that suits your fancy. Each typeface has a "personality," but the ones that I've included on page 120 are both rather bold and very legible, even from a distance (which is an important feature for a banner). For my "Welcome Home" I used the computer to manipulate the lettering—somewhat more extended for the short words and more condensed for the longer words (see photo at right). I did this in order to make all of the words the same length, which gives the banner a cohesive look.

PREPARING THE DOWELS

Cut two dowels for the basic "Welcome Home" banner according to the dimensions indicated in the Materials Needed list. (If you make a different-sized banner, adjust the size of the dowels.) Sand the dowels and paint them with gesso (see

Since some of the words in my banner were longer or shorter than others, I used the computer to condense or extend the letters in order to make the type fit.

photo below). After drying, sand them again and paint them with a second coat of gesso. After drying, sand them and paint them with a coat of red acrylic paint. After drying, sand them. Then paint them with a final coat of red acrylic paint, add an upholstery tack to each end, and set them aside until they are needed in Step 14.

Before painting, prepare the dowels by sanding them.

Stitching "Welcome Home"

NOTE As with all the projects, you may enlarge or reduce the pattern to whatever size suits you. The instructions below are for a basic banner that is 29¹/2" x 16". To create the basic "Welcome Home" banner, enlarge the "Welcome Home" Banner pattern that appears on page 119 to 29¹/2" x 16" (or to whatever size suits you). If you need more detailed information on creating stitched artwork from a pattern, refer back to Steps 1 to 11 on pages 40 to 49. Then follow the instructions below to complete the project.

STEP 1

In choosing your fabrics, consider that nylon canvas is more opaque and stiffer than ripstop nylon fabric. Therefore, a banner made with nylon canvas will have more "body" than one made with ripstop nylon. However, I found that nylon canvas is not readily available in most fabric stores. Both are water-resistant, which makes them suitable for hanging both outdoors and indoors. (Only a synthetic fabric such as nylon can withstand rain and snow. Other fabrics will be damaged by the elements.)

Both of these nylon fabrics come in a rather limited number of colors (see photo above right). I chose red, white, yellow, and turquoise. For your version of the "Welcome Home" banner, choose colors that appeal to you and that work well with one another.

STEP 2

Make your final fabric choices by juxtaposing fabrics on top of the pattern. Then create a rough fabric paste-up. (If you need help in creating a rough fabric paste-up, see page 42 for instructions.) Or you can use colored pencils to decide on the color layout (see photo at far right). I decided on red and white for the stripes and loops, yellow for the rectangular sections, and turquoise for the lettering.

STEP 3

Based on your rough fabric paste-up or colored pencil sketch, steampress the nylon fabrics using a cool setting on your iron. It would be helpful to use fusible webbing to fuse the letters in place. However, with the higher setting on your iron that is needed for the fusible webbing, the nylon fabric would then pucker. Instead, to keep the letters in place, try "Heat-and-Steam" fusible webbing that has a sticky adhesive surface.

Another option is to use polyester twill iron-on polyester fabric backed with heat-seal film. The back of this fabric is pretreated and you can fuse the fabric in position just by ironing it down (see "Resources").

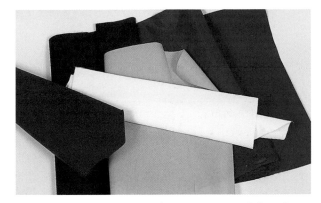

These were some of the color choices available in nylon canvas fabric (see Step 1).

> **HINT**
> If you want to create a banner that is meant for indoor use only, consider using felt or other fabrics for your "Welcome Home" banner.

This rough sketch was the beginning of "Welcome Home" banner (see Step 2).

Here's the colored pencil sketch that I did when deciding on the color layout for my banner (see Step 2).

STEP 4

In this step you will be tracing and cutting out the shapes of the "Welcome Home" banner.

Yellow Sections Tape your pattern on the light box *right side up*. Tape the yellow fabric on top of the pattern. Use a Pigma Micron pen to trace the rectangular sections from the pattern onto the front of your fabric pieces. (Though the ink of these pens is normally permanent, when used on the nylon fabric the ink may be washed out later.) Add $1/4$" extra fabric on all sides to hem each section later in Step 5.

House Area Tape your pattern on the light box *wrong side up*. Place the white fabric on top of the pattern. Use a Pigma Micron pen to trace the shape from the pattern onto the back of your fabric, allowing $1/8$" extra on the white fabric where the red roof shape should overlap the house shape (refer to the photo below left if you need help). Tape and trace the red fabric.

Red Pieces With a Pigma Micron pen, trace five $2^1/2$"-x-18"-long pieces onto the front surface of the red nylon fabric. Within each piece, draw a $7/16$" hemline on the left and right sides along the 18" dimension of the fabric.

White Pieces Follow the same instructions as for the red pieces, but trace *four* $2^1/2$"-x-18" pieces onto the front surface of the white nylon fabric.

Red Edgings for the Yellow Sections Use a Pigma Micron pen to trace two 1"-x-36" pieces onto the red fabric.

Cut out all of the pieces of fabric you have traced or drawn above. Place the two 1"-x-36" pieces of red fabric *right side down* on the sticky board (see page 47 to learn how to make a sticky board).

Here's what the house section looks like with all the fabric pieces in place.

STEP 5

On each rectangular yellow section, turn under a 1/4" hem and machine-sew a running stitch. On the long sides of the red and white pieces, turn under a 7/16" hem and machine-sew a running stitch 1/8" from the edge on the front surface.

STEP 6

After you have chosen your typeface, use a copier machine or your computer to enlarge the alphabet to the size that you envision for your lettering. Then use a black Pentel marker to trace the letters needed for your words onto a piece of vellum, making a separate lettering pattern for each traced word. Fold the vellum in half to find the center of each word. Tape down each lettering pattern on the light box *wrong side up*. Trace the shapes of the letters onto the *wrong side* of the polyester twill iron-on polyester fabric or nylon fabric that you have chosen for your lettering.

STEP 7

Cut out the letters and position them *wrong side up* on the sticky board.

STEP 8

Lightly spray them with spray adhesive.

STEP 9

For each yellow section, tape its corresponding lettering pattern *right side up* on the light box. Then center the hemmed yellow section *right side up* on top of the pattern and position the letters in place on top of the yellow section.

Next, position the shapes for the house onto its yellow section.

STEP 10

If you used polyester twill iron-on polyester fabric for your lettering, fuse the letters down by carefully ironing them in place using a tacking iron or the tip of your iron, set on a medium heat. *Be careful not to iron the nylon fabric because the heat will pucker the fabric.* If you used nylon

HINT

For an interesting contrast, after zigzag-stitching the house shapes, add a decorative blanket stitch using the opposing color (red stitching on the white shape and white stitching on the red shapes (see photo above right).

Here's what the house section of the "Welcome Home" banner looks like with decorative stitching added to the house area.

fabric for the letters, do not iron them. The adhesive will hold them in place.

STEP 11

Machine-sew the shapes and letters down with a zigzag stitch using matching *rayon or nylon thread* (see photo above right). If you use polycotton thread for *outside* banners, weather conditions will dry out the thread and it will break off.

On the front of the left and right sides of all of the yellow sections, pin a length of the 1" red fabric strip that you had cut out in Step 4. Put 1/2" of the red strip on the front and fold the other 1/2" to the back. Zigzag-stitch it in place and then machine-sew a running stitch 1/8" along the edge (see diagram at right).

This diagram shows how the 1" piece of red edging is folded over and then stitched on the left and right sides of each yellow area (see Step 11).

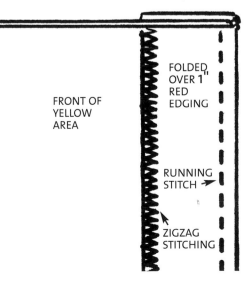

FRONT OF YELLOW AREA

FOLDED OVER 1" RED EDGING

RUNNING STITCH →

ZIGZAG STITCHING

STEP 12

Place the "Welcome Home" Banner pattern on the light box *right side up*. Tape tear-away paper on top of the entire pattern.

From a file folder, cut out two rectangles, one that is 1⁵/8" x 6" and one that is 1⁵/8" x 2¹/2". Use them to measure ten 6" pieces and ten 2¹/2" pieces of the hemmed red pieces in Step 4. Measure eight 6" pieces and eight 2¹/2" pieces of the four hemmed white pieces. Cut out the pieces. (The 6" pieces will be used for making the loops on the top and bottom of the banner. The 2¹/2" pieces will be used for the stripes above and below the house section.)

Using white artist's tape and straight pins, follow the "Welcome Home" Banner pattern and secure the pieces onto the tear-away paper. Fold the pieces of 6" red and white hemmed fabric to form loops and, using the light box and the pattern, alternate the loops in position at the top and bottom of the banner. Center the 2¹/2" stripes with an equal amount of each stripe overlapping the top and bottom of the house section. Then tape and pin the yellow sections so that they overlap the stripes and loops.

STEP 13

Using matching thread, machine-sew a running stitch over the yellow sections, the red edges, the tear-away paper, the loops, and the stripes. On the loops below the HOME section, machine-sew a running stitch 1¹/8" up from the bottom of the loops (see photo above left). On the loops above the WELCOME section, machine-sew a running stitch 1¹/8" down from the top of the loops. Use matching red and white threads. (These stitched channels are where the dowels will slide through.)

After you have completed your sewing, trim off any extra fabric from the back of the banner (see photo above left). If the Pigma Micron lines that you drew in Step 4 are visible, dip the banner in sudsy water to remove the lines. Rinse and hang it up to dry.

STEP 14

To position the dowels for the basic "Welcome Home" banner, insert red dowels through the banner's top loops and bottom loops.

If you are adding a personalized name banner (see "Personalizing the Banner" on page 73), attach it using the S-shaped hooks. Insert a dowel in the bottom loops of the name section. Attach cord or ribbon to the ends of the top dowel. Display your banner!

Trim the excess fabric from the back of the banner (see Step 13).

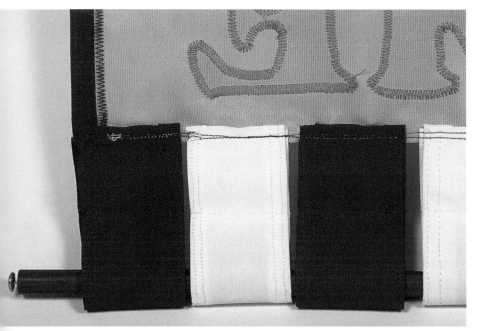

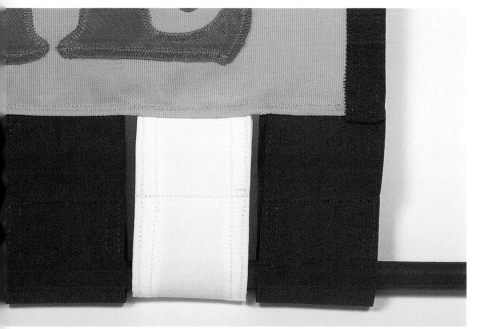

Insert the dowels through the top and bottom loops of the banner (see Step 14).

Personalizing the Banner

PERSONALIZED NAME SECTIONS

To make each name section, use the "Personalized Name Section" pattern that appears on page 120 and follow the instructions below.

YELLOW SECTION FOR EACH PERSONALIZED NAME SECTION

Trace the "Personalized Name Section" pattern that appears on page 120 onto yellow fabric as you did in Step 4 on page 70. Fold over a $1/4$" hem on all sides of the rectangle. Prepare the lettering as in Steps 6 to 11 on page 71.

LOOPS FOR EACH PERSONALIZED NAME SECTION

Follow the instructions in Step 4 on page 70 to prepare five 6" red pieces and four 6" white pieces. Arrange them as loops behind the yellow section as in Step 12 on page 72. Machine-sew the loops in place with a running stitch.

HOOKS

For each name section, make four S-shaped hooks from coated red wire. (The S-Shaped Hook pattern appears on page 120.) Stitch the S-shaped hooks onto the back of the name section. Attach the S-shaped hooks sewn to the back of the name section over the bottom dowel of the basic banner. Add a dowel through the name section's loops.

By adding any of the personalized name sections, the basic "Welcome Home" banner grows to 37" x 16" and welcomes home either our daughter, Kate; Frank; or myself.

The banner is a colorful homecoming message.

Hangings

All of the appliquéd artwork in this gallery was commissioned, either by individuals, galleries, or corporations. Unlike most of my other work, these pieces were not meant to be used as illustration. Instead, they were intended to hang on the wall. Much of the work is large in scale. Another difference is that while my illustration commissions have very short deadlines (a week or two), I was given a much longer period of time to work on these commissioned hangings: in some cases, up to two years.

Lobster
36" x 36"; part of "Hands"
144" x 108" (1992)
Margaret Cusack, "Hands," Stitched Art Installation. Collection of The Culinary Institute of America.

Wine
36" x 36"; part of "Hands"
144" x 108" (1992)
Margaret Cusack, "Hands," Stitched Art Installation. Collection of The Culinary Institute of America.

Tomato
36" x 36"; part of "Hands"
144" x 108" (1992)
Margaret Cusack, "Hands," Stitched Art Installation. Collection of The Culinary Institute of America.

Vegetables
(Harvest Series) 108" x 60" (1976)
Commissioned by George Nelson for Thrivent Financial for Lutherans (Formerly Aid Association for Lutherans)

Apples
(Harvest Series) 108" x 60" (1976)
Commissioned by George Nelson for Thrivent Financial for Lutherans (Formerly Aid Association for Lutherans)

Corn
(Harvest Series) 108" x 60" (1976)
Commissioned by George Nelson for Thrivent Financial for Lutherans (Formerly Aid Association for Lutherans)

Skeist Skyscape
54" x 104" (1979)
Commissioned by
and Collection of
Marian Skeist.

George Washington
33" x 25" (1982)

A Question of Balance
20" x 28" (1998)
Commissioned by and Collection of
Women's Alliance of the First
Unitarian Congregation of Brooklyn

A Time for Hope
72" x 144" (1994)
"A Time for Hope" stitched
artwork commissioned for
the lobby of Bishop Francis J.
Mugavero Center for Geriatric
Care—Saint Vincent Catholic
Medical Centers of New York.
Architect: Joseph Marino.
Year Created: 1994.
Permission Granted: 2005.

*"There is a right physical
size for every idea."*
HENRY MOORE

CHAPTER 6

Using Selective Padding

Flowers are such a universal theme, taking in everything from Van Gogh's multi-million dollar *Irises* to simple greeting cards and children's drawings. And images of flowers have such a profound effect on us. As paintings in museums or even artwork in hospital hallways, flowers can be solemn, cheerful, uplifting, and poignant—often, all at the same time. With a few brushstrokes, an Asian sumi flower painting is as meaningful as it is delicate. And yet Georgia O'Keeffe's paintings of flowers are as dynamic and engineered as her structured images of bridges and buildings. As you can see by the bright colors and energy of "Vase of Flowers," I was channeling Frida Kahlo and Henri Matisse, as well as all of you who, like me, simply love flowers.

With "Vase of Flowers" and this chapter, we'll explore adding dimension to fabric artwork by inserting padding *only* in specific areas.

Vase of Flowers
24" x 18" (2004)

Stitching "Vase of Flowers"

MATERIALS NEEDED

In addition to the materials in the General Materials Needed lists on pages 30 and 40, you will need the following:

assorted floral fabrics

Images of flowers are everywhere.

Over the years, I've amassed a wonderful collection of fabrics with flower motifs. And, as you will see, I've used quite a few of them in this project.

Usually, I start a project by doing research and creating sketches. However, with "Vase of Flowers" I started with the floral fabrics themselves and then let the sizes of the flowers determine the final dimensions of the artwork. As you begin this project, consider the *sizes* of the flowers in your floral fabrics. You may decide that, instead of 24" x 18" as a finished size, you want to enlarge or reduce the pattern to a proportion that works best for *your* flowers.

Follow the instructions below to complete the "Vase of Flowers" artwork. If you need more detailed information on creating stitched artwork from a pattern, refer back to Steps 1 to 11 on pages 40 to 49.

STEP 1

Enlarge the "Vase of Flowers" pattern that appears on page 121 to the size that relates best to the flowers that you've chosen. Select a variety of fabrics for each of the shapes in the pattern.

> *"I found I could say things with color and shapes that I couldn't say in any other way—things that I had no words for."*
> GEORGIA O'KEEFFE

STEP 2

Make your final fabric choices by juxtaposing fabrics on top of your pattern. For "Vase of Flowers" I used flowers from eight different fabrics (see photo on facing page). You should decide for yourself which of your flowers will complement the others and add up to a beautiful "bouquet." As you can see, my color choices were a buttercup yellow for the background, a burgundy print for the table, a blue lace for the vase, an earthy green for the stems and leaves, and a quiltlike print fabric for the border.

Choose the colors for the fabrics for your "Vase of Flowers"—the background, table, vase, stems, leaves, flowers, and border.

Then create a rough fabric paste-up of your chosen fabrics. (If you need help in creating a rough fabric paste-up, see page 42.)

After you have chosen your fabrics and flowers, it's important to have an actual structure for positioning the flower shapes within the composition. Enlarge the "Vase of Flowers" Stem

HINT

Consider using floral fabrics left over from clothing, drapes, or slipcovers that you've made. This will add a personal touch to your finished project. Choose the flowers that most appeal to you and those that work best with one another.

When choosing your fabrics, you should also consider the color scheme of your particular flowers and the colors in the room where your "Vase of Flowers" will hang once it's completed.

"Nature never lets you down."
DAVID HOCKNEY

The individual flowers for "Vase of Flowers" were cut from these eight fabrics (see Step 3).

Structure pattern that appears on page 121 and use the stems in the pattern as a basis for positioning your flower and leaf shapes. Adding these shapes on top of the stems' structure will more than likely cover up most of the stems. However, having the stem structure underneath your flowers will make the finished artwork look more realistic.

STEP 3

Based on your rough fabric paste-up, cut out generous pieces of your chosen fabrics. Set your iron on "cotton" and press them, using spray starch and ironing the fabrics on the back. Next, iron paper-backed fusible webbing onto the backs of your fabric pieces, taking care not to iron the fusible webbing onto your ironing board surface.

STEP 4

Cut out the flower shapes. Trace all the other shapes shown on the pattern onto the backs of your fabric pieces. Remember to add an extra 1/8" to each shape in the background that underlaps the shapes in the foreground. The diagram at right shows the sequence of overlapping shapes in "Vase of Flowers."

STEP 5

Cut out the backing fabric. As before, set your iron on "cotton" and press the fabric, using spray starch.

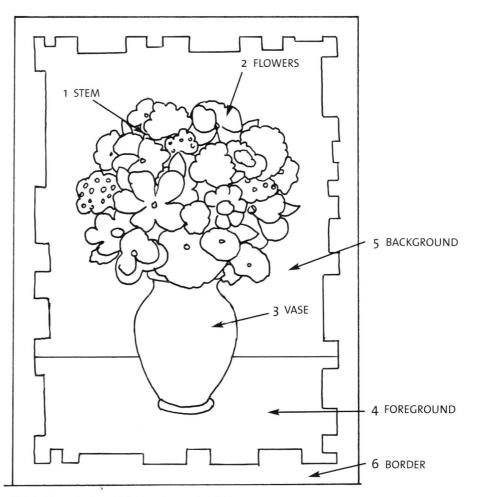

This is the order in which the shapes should be traced: first the stems; next the flowers; and then the vase, the foreground, the background, and the border (see Step 4).

Draw a padding shape on acetate for each fabric shape that you want to pad. Make sure that the padding shape is 3/8" smaller than your fabric shape (see Step 6).

HINT
If you decide not to do the padded effect, there's another option: Just fuse down your fabric shapes in Step 10 and don't stitch them at all. However, if you do add the padding, it's best to stitch down all the edges since it would be difficult to keep your fused, padded shapes in place if they weren't stitched down.

STEP 6

With "Vase of Flowers" I used a selective padding technique (adding dimension to some or all of the shapes). I padded the vase and all of the flowers. You can decide for yourself which shapes to pad in your artwork.

To add padding to your shapes, choose either batting or felt. Batting is useful for large areas, but it's more difficult to cut precise small shapes. Felt is not as thick, but it's easier to cut out very defined shapes.

Cut out enough padding to cover the area of your flower bouquet. Iron fusible webbing to the back of your padding.

Turn over your pattern (and your shapes that are to be padded) so that you are seeing them from the back. Place acetate over the back of the shape. Using a Sharpee marker, draw an outline on the acetate that is 3/8" smaller than the original shape (see photo above left). Transfer the new shape onto the back of the padding and set it aside to be cut out in Step 7.

STEP 7

Cut out the shapes (see photo below). Position the shapes on the sticky board *wrong side up*. (If you need help to make a sticky board, see page 47 for instructions.)

HINT
When you position the padding shape under the corresponding fabric shape, you will notice that the fabric shape will extend over the padding. Don't worry. When the padding and fabric are fused down and stitched, the padding will provide just the right amount of dimension to the shape.

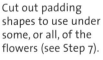

Cut out padding shapes to use under some, or all, of the flowers (see Step 7).

STEP 8

Remove the paper backing of the fusible webbing from the backs of the cut shapes. Lightly spray the backs of the shapes with spray adhesive.

STEP 9

Tape the pattern *right side up* on the light box. Tape the backing fabric over it and, following the pattern, position the fabric shapes onto the backing fabric. Add the padding shapes underneath their corresponding fabric shapes (see photo top right).

STEP 10

Set your iron on "cotton" and fuse the shapes down by ironing them in place. Because the padding creates an irregular surface, it's best to use the tip of your iron to carefully press down all the edges of the fabric shapes that include padding (see photo center right).

STEP 11

Machine-sew the shapes down with a zigzag stitch (see photo bottom right).

STEP 12

Add embellishments, decorative stitching, or whatever you like. Then complete your "Vase of Flowers" by making it into a hanging or pillow. You could also staple it onto canvas stretchers, wood, or foam core and frame it.

"No amount of skillful invention can replace the essential element of imagination."
EDWARD HOPPER

Position the padded shapes under the fabric shapes (see Step 9).

Using the tip of your iron is best for fusing down the edges (see Step 10).

Use a zigzag stitch to sew down your shapes (see Step 11).

Still Lifes

Still life imagery has always interested me. Perhaps it's because I like to cook and I enjoy food. With my fabric collection, I have limitless possibilities of matching up the color and textures of food with the fabrics that I have on hand: smooth red satin for tomatoes, ribbed corduroy for celery—the possibilities are endless.

Peek Freans Chocolate Chips
19" x 15" (1984)
Commissioned by Kraft Foods Holdings, Inc. for Peek Freans Biscuits ad

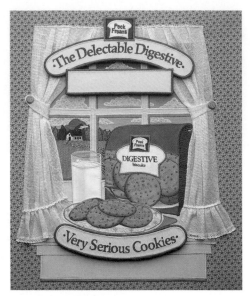

Peek Freans Digestive
24" x 21" (1984)
Commissioned by Kraft Foods Holdings, Inc. for Peek Freans Biscuits ad

Peek Freans Shortcake
20" x 16" (1984)
Commissioned by Kraft Foods Holdings, Inc. for Peek Freans Biscuits ad

October Still Life
16" x 14" (1985)
Commissioned by Avon Products, Inc. for 1986 Centennial Avon calendar

Fish on a Plate
12" x 18" (1973)

Peaches and Dahlias
13" x 16" (1983)
Commissioned by and Collection of
Jack and Bernadette Sidebotham.

*"The day is coming when a
single carrot freshly observed
will set off a revolution."*
PAUL CEZANNE

Bloomingdale's at Home
15" x 11" (1974)
Reproduced with permission
of Bloomingdale's, Inc.

Uncle Ben's Still Life
11" x 25" (1987)
Commissioned by Rives, Smith, Baldwin,
Carlberg and Y & R for Uncle Ben's Rice
canister. It is used with permission.

CATHERINE & HAROLD

PATRICIA

JAMES

JOANN

MARGARET

BARBARA

DEBORAH

WEAVER FAMILY

CHAPTER 7

Using Overall Padding

In Chapter 6 padding was used under only some of the shapes. However, this project, "Family Tree" hanging, introduces the technique of overall padding (using padding under *all* of the shapes, creating a quilted effect).

Family trees hark back to Shaker imagery and the folk art tradition of creating an artful document that shows a family's genealogical history. If you make a "Family Tree" for yourself, you might want to get printed fabric copies of it for each person included in your "tree." Besides basing a "Family Tree" on your own relatives, you might also decide to make a "Friends Tree" with the names of your close friends. Or perhaps a "Pet Tree" that would include the names of the favorite animals in your life!

(To explain my "Family Tree" shown here: My maiden name is Weaver, and this tree includes my parents, five siblings, and myself.)

Family Tree
24" x 18" (2005)

Stitching "Family Tree"

MATERIALS NEEDED

❧

In addition to the materials in the General Materials Needed lists on pages 30 and 40, you will need the following:

lightweight interfacing, approximately 36" x 36"

acrylic paint
(choose colors for the labels' lettering and borders)

❧

I used different patterned fabrics to create the rolling hills in "Family Tree." This added an illusion of depth to the artwork.

Follow the instructions below to complete the "Family Tree" hanging. If you need more detailed information on creating stitched artwork from a pattern, refer back to Steps 1 to 11 on pages 40 to 49.

STEP 1

Decide on how many labels you will need for your "tree" and then enlarge one of the "Family Tree" patterns that appear on pages 122 and 123 to the size you wish. Choose a variety of fabrics for each of the shapes in the pattern.

STEP 2

Make your final fabric choices by juxtaposing fabrics on top of your pattern. Then create a rough fabric paste-up of your chosen fabrics. (If you need help in creating a rough fabric paste-up, see page 42.)

STEP 3

Based on your rough fabric paste-up, cut out generous pieces of your chosen fabrics. Set your iron on "cotton" and press them, using spray starch and ironing the fabric on the back. Next, iron paper-backed fusible webbing onto the backs of

your fabric pieces, taking care not to iron the fusible webbing onto your ironing board surface.

STEP 4

Tape your pattern onto the light box *wrong side up*. Trace the shapes from the pattern onto the paper backing of the fusible webbing. (To make the labels, see "Making the Labels" on pages 89 to 90.)

STEP 5

Cut out the cotton duck backing fabric, adding an extra $1^1/2$" to all of the outside edges. Set your iron on "cotton" and press the fabric using spray starch. It will be used in Step 10.

STEP 6

To have a quiltlike, overall padded effect for your artwork, cut out a piece of lightweight, white batiste fabric that is $1^1/2$" larger on all sides than the size of your pattern. (Batiste fabric is used rather than a heavier fabric because in Step 10 you will "sandwich" a layer of batting between it and the cotton duck backing fabric. The stitching in Step 11 will create a quilted effect in the finished artwork.)

Also cut out a layer of batting 1" larger than the size of your pattern and set it aside. Iron fusible webbing onto the back of the batiste fabric. *Do not remove the paper backing.*

STEP 7

Cut out the shapes and position them *wrong side up* on the sticky board. (If you need help to make a sticky board, see page 47 for instructions.)

STEP 8

Remove the paper backing of the fusible webbing from the backs of the labels and the other fabric shapes. Lightly spray them with spray adhesive.

STEP 9

Tape the pattern *right side up* on the light box. Tape the lightweight cotton batiste fabric on top of the pattern and position the fabric shapes on it (see photo above right).

At times it's helpful to have an additional acetate or tracing paper copy of the pattern to tape on top of the artwork to check the position of the shapes, or use the original pattern to check your shapes' positions (see photo below right).

There's also another way to help in positioning the shapes: When you are cutting out a shape that is underneath (such as the tree and its branches), include the shapes that will later overlap it. For example, in the photograph above right you'll see that when the tree trunk fabric was cut out, the label areas were included in the tree trunk fabric. This helped in positioning the labels and leaves correctly.

> HINT
>
> When you are choosing fabrics for "Family Tree," consider using colorful ones. To create a landscape and a tree such as the ones in this project, you will find that there are many fabrics available at your fabric stores that relate to the clouds, tree trunk, grass, leaves, and sky.

Position the shapes on top of the batiste fabric. When I traced the shape for the tree fabric, I included the leaf and label shapes with the overall tree shape. This made it easier to position the leaves and labels (see Step 9).

Putting the pattern on top of the project can be helpful when checking the position of the shapes (see Step 9).

STEP 10

Fuse the fabric shapes in place by ironing them onto the batiste fabric. Then remove the paper backing from the batiste fabric. Lightly spray adhesive onto the top of the cotton duck backing fabric, which will be the bottom layer of the "sandwich" shown in the photo at left. Then put the backing fabric *adhesive side up* on your ironing board.

Lightly spray adhesive onto the layer of batting (this was cut slightly smaller than the backing fabric). Position it *adhesive side up* on top of the backing fabric. Then put the batiste fabric (with all the shapes fused in place) *right side up* on top of the batting. You now have a "sandwich" of the two fabrics with the batting inside (see photo at left). You can also check yourself by referring to the diagram

on page 48.) Put this "sandwich" on the ironing board, cover it with a pressing cloth, set your iron on "cotton," and lightly iron it all together.

If needed, use long straight pins to hold everything in place. You are now ready to sew down all the shapes.

STEP 11

Machine-sew the shapes down with a zigzag stitch.

STEP 12

Add embellishments, decorative stitching, or whatever you like. Then complete your "Family Tree" by making it into a hanging. You could also make it into a pillow or staple it onto canvas stretchers, wood, or foam core and frame it (see photo below right).

Another option for finishing this project is to stitch on a border fabric to bind the edges as you would a quilt. Then sew a narrow fabric sleeve onto the back (see diagram below left). Insert a rod in the sleeve so that "Family Tree" can be hung on the wall.

Here's what your three-layered "sandwich" looks like—top layer: the batiste fabric (with all of the fabric shapes fused on it); middle layer: the batting; bottom layer: the cotton duck backing fabric (see Step 10).

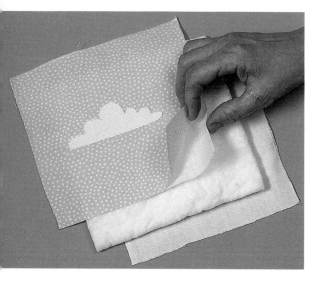

To make "Family Tree" into a quilted hanging, stitch a narrow fabric sleeve onto the back of the project and insert a rod through it (see Step 12).

FABRIC SLEEVE

BACK OF
"FAMILY TREE"

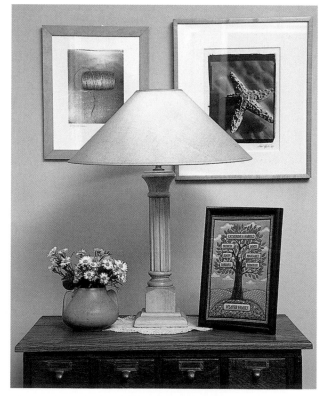

This is a framed fabric print of "Family Tree" (see Step 12).

Making the Labels

Before making the labels, you should consider both their size and their position on "Family Tree." To help, I've included four patterns. The one on page 122 has no labels, the ones on page 123 show label positions for seven, eight, and nine labels. Enlarge whichever pattern fits the needs of your artwork.

POSITIONING THE LABELS

Enlarge the Label Border patterns that appear on page 123. Make copies of the patterns and place them on the "Family Tree" pattern that has no labels. (This will help you decide what looks best for how you envision your "Family Tree.") Use as many labels as you like. However, if you have more labels than are shown on the "Weaver Family Tree," consider making the labels smaller. If you like, include a title or name label in the area below the tree, as I did.

When designing your own "tree/label" composition, decide where your labels will be positioned, then delete the leaf and tree branch shapes from under the label areas, allowing for an underlap for the shapes that will underlap each label or leaf. If you neglect to do this, you may end up with lumps underneath your labels.

PERSONALIZING THE LABELS

To personalize your hanging with labels, you can paint, write, machine-stitch, or embroider the names onto fabric labels and then sew the labels onto your "Family Tree" in Step 11 on page 88. Another option is to have each person write his or her name on a piece of fabric and make it into a label (see top photo on page 90). Or, instead of names, have photographs of your subjects printed onto fabric and then incorporate the photos into your "tree." Having the

This is an example of the embroidered lettering.

names personalized will enrich the "Family Tree" and make it even more of an heirloom. If you decide to do this, follow the instructions below.

Painted Labels Use the computer to print out the lettering for each name at the size that you wish it to appear on the label. You can also print out the letters by hand. Tape the lettering *right side up* on the light box. Prepare the fabric for the labels (see Step 3 on page 86). Put your prepared fabric *right side up* on top of the lettering. Using a thin Micron marker, trace the outline of the lettering onto the fabric, leaving enough room around each name to add the label's border. With a fine brush and acrylic paint, fill in the outlined lettering.

If you want, you may also leave the painted names as they are or stitch them as discussed on page 90.

"A kiss from my mother made me a painter."
BENJAMIN WEST

HINT
Before positioning your labels in Step 9 on pages 87, take a look at "Other Uses for the 'Family Tree' Artwork" on page 91. An option at this stage is to stitch just the tree, leaves, clouds, and landscape. Then, before adding the labels, get fabric print copies of your artwork. (See "Printed Fabric Projects" on pages 62 to 63.) You can then use the fabric copies to make additional "Family Trees" using different names on each one.

Autographed Labels Instead of using printed lettering, have each person write his or her name on fabric using a permanent marker (see photo top left). You can leave the autographed labels as they are. However, if you wish to stitch them, follow the directions on this page.

Adding Borders to the Labels Every label needs a border, and if you plan to stitch your names, the borders should be drawn in place before the stitching begins. Use the Label Border patterns to create a border for each label. Copy or trace both the left- and right-hand sections and overlap them on your light box to accommodate the length of each name.

With all the labels, tape the label pattern onto the light box. Center each name over the label pattern and use a thin Micron marker to trace the shape of the label's border around each name. Adjust the length of the label according to the length of each name (see photo center left). Then carefully fill in the borders of the labels with acrylic paint.

Machine-Stitched or Embroidered Labels Having stitched names enriches the "Family Tree" and will make it even more special (see photo bottom left). If you decide to do this, follow these instructions.

Iron fusible webbing onto the back of the labels' fabric. Peel off the paper backing and fuse a lightweight interfacing onto the back of the fabric. This will keep the fabric from puckering and will give it more "body" since the stitching will "stress" the fabric.

To *machine-stitch* the names, use a tight zigzag stitch. If you choose to *hand-embroider* the names, first stretch the fabric on an embroidery hoop or onto canvas stretchers. NOTE Do not stitch the labels' borders at this point.

When the stitching is complete, iron another layer of fusible webbing onto the back of the entire label's fabric. Then carefully cut out each label at the outside edge of the borders and set them all aside for use in Step 8 on page 86.

Labels may be autographed.

Overlap the two sides of the Label Border pattern to accommodate the size of each name.

The "Weaver Family" printed lettering was traced onto fabric and the lettering was hand-embroidered. The border was later machine-stitched onto the artwork.

Other Uses for the Artwork

ADDITIONAL HANGINGS

Stitch your hanging (without *any* labels) and then have several copies of it printed onto paper-backed fabric at your photocopy store. Prepare your labels and stitch them directly onto the fabric copies instead of onto the original project. In that way you may use many copies of this original stitched artwork to create a variety of hangings for different families and/or groups of friends, all based on the original stitched (but label*less*) "Family Tree."

SCRAPBOOK COVER

To turn your "Family Tree" hanging into a scrapbook cover, get smaller color copies of your hanging made at your local copy store, either on paper or paper-backed fabric. Incorporate each copy into the cover of the scrapbook or album as gifts for family and friends.

FRAMED PRINTS

Make printed-fabric copies of your stitched artwork, and then frame them. They make thoughtful gifts that your family and friends are sure to cherish.

Here's what a copy of "Family Tree" printed on fabric looks like as the cover of a 13^1/2"-x-11" scrapbook.

This fabric print of "Family Tree" has been framed. In front of it is an additional fabric print on the left and a paper print on the right.

Quilted Images

These quilted images harken back to the early American appliquéd quilts that told a sequential story in the quilt's rectangles. Besides the narrative and the dimensional aspects of quilted imagery, I'm intrigued by quilts' inherent qualities of nurturing and hand-made warmth.

Coming Home
14" x 13" (2001)
Commissioned by *The Chicago Tribune*

Harcourt Checkerboard Quilt
14" x 11" (1982)
Commissioned by Harcourt, Inc. Reproduced by permission of the publisher.

American Songbook
(1990)
Commissioned by The Hearst Corporation

"Nature is so much richer than anything you can imagine."
GEORGE TOOKER

Topsy Turvy
15¹/2" x 12" (2002)
Commissioned for *America West* Magazine

(Family Tree) Three Volt Family Values
24" x 18" (1992)
Commissioned by and Collection of
Atmel Corporation.

Absolut Pennsylvania
28" x 34" (2002)
Commissioned by G2NY for Absolut Vodka poster.
Courtesy of V&S Absolut Spirits.

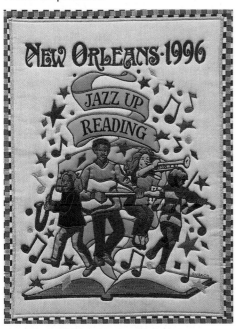

Jazz Up Reading
24" x 15" (1996)
Commissioned by The McGraw-Hill
Companies, Inc. for poster

**Parental
Bequests**
14" x 9" (1985)
Commissioned
by G+J USA
Publishing for
Parents
Magazine

Book Quilt
24" x 48" (1990)
Commissioned by Simon &
Schuster, Inc./Prentice Hall Press
for catalog cover

CHAPTER 8

Working from a Photograph

This fabric artwork, "Nostalgic Portrait," was created for a friend, Jim Vacirca, who commissioned me to stitch a fiftieth-wedding anniversary gift for his parents. The result, "Nostalgic Portrait," is an image based on the 1933 wedding photograph of Ida and Anthony Vacirca. (You can see a copy of the original photo on page 101.)

When I saw the photograph, I was very moved by the faces of Jim's parents, which were so evocative and full of promise. I'm always impressed by the charm and inherent dignity of these kinds of images. For many people, photographs of family and friends can evoke warm feelings, affectionate memories, and sometimes even feelings of sadness over the loss of loved ones. Creating artwork based on *your* old photos can reconcile family memories, focus your emotions, and perhaps be a comfort to you and your family. This chapter will show you how.

Nostalgic Portrait
31" x 20" (1983)
Commissioned by James Vacirca.
Collection of Darlene and Gary Cooper.

Designing Your Pattern

MATERIALS NEEDED

☙

In addition to the materials in the General Materials Needed lists on pages 30 and 40, you will need the following:

photographs

manila folder

metal ruler

☙

I find that even anonymous antique photographs can be charming. The people in them seem to want to tell their story. So if you want to do a nostalgic portrait but can't settle on an image of someone you know, you might want to "adopt" one of these orphaned photographs and base your image on a photograph that "calls out" to you from an antique store, garage sale, or flea market.

In this chapter, you will learn how to design and stitch a unique "Nostalgic Portrait" of your own—either using a cherished photograph or an anonymous one. Or, if you like, re-create my version of "Nostalgic Portrait" by enlarging the pattern that appears on page 124. If you need more detailed information on creating stitched artwork from a pattern, refer back to Steps 1 to 11 on page 40 to 49.

To design your own image, choose a photograph and then enlarge it to the size that you envision for your finished artwork. The next steps are to crop the photograph and trace it to create your pattern. The following instructions will lead you through the steps of designing your own pattern. If you need more detailed information on designing, refer to Step 1, "Designing Your Image," on pages 30 to 32, especially the section that deals with working from photographs.

Even contemporary photographs can be the subject of a nostalgic portrait.

> **HINT**
> You can also choose a contemporary photograph such as one of the photos pictured above and make it nostalgic by using brown and beige fabrics, thereby creating an old-fashioned sepia-toned effect as I did in "Nostalgic Portrait."

STEP 1
CHOOSING YOUR
PHOTOGRAPH

When designing an image, do research and make small rough sketches. Choose your favorite sketch and refine it in pencil on tracing paper. Since your pattern will be based mainly on a photograph, you do not have to be an expert at drawing.

Look over your family photographs and choose a favorite image. (It will remain unharmed during this project.) It could be a photo of your mother as a young child, your parents and you at your graduation, a snapshot of your entire family on a favorite vacation, your dog, your grandparents holding you as a baby— whatever suits you (see the photo above for examples).

When making your final decision, look for a photograph where your subjects' faces are *in focus*. When deciding on which photo to use, base your decision on the images of the people, not the surroundings, because in the final analysis, the background will probably be less important than the faces of the people.

Old photographs present a wealth of possibilities for stitched art projects.

HINT
As you develop your sketch, you may decide to simplify the image by eliminating some of the buildings or the less important figures.

To design the final shape of your project, use the croppers to focus in on the most important area of the photograph (see Step 2).

STEP 2
CROPPING YOUR PHOTOGRAPH

Once you have chosen your photograph, you may wish to crop the image so that you can focus on the area that interests you. For example, if your photo includes your grandmother as a child in front of a large house, you might want to eliminate much of the house so that you concentrate on the image of your grandmother.

You can crop your photograph either manually or on your computer.

To *crop your photograph manually*, carefully tape the photograph to a piece of lightweight cardboard. Then tape a piece of acetate on top of the photo to protect it. (In this way, it will remain unharmed.)

Place a pair of croppers on top of the acetate that covers your photograph. (See "Making Croppers," below, for help in making a pair.) To decide how much of the image to use, experiment by moving the croppers in and out, making a larger or smaller rectangle. Focus in on the area of the photograph that most appeals to you (see photo at left).

When you are satisfied with the results, tape the croppers in position. At your local photocopy store, enlarge the cropped image to whatever size you wish for the finished artwork. (Most copy stores are able to enlarge images up to 36" x 48"). If the store offers an option of lightening or darkening the enlargement, request that it be made lighter. It will then be easier to understand the shapes of light and shadow in Step 3 on page 99 if the image is somewhat lighter.

To *crop your photograph on your computer*, scan the photograph and import it into the computer. Then manipulate it to improve contrast and sharpness. Simplify the image, if you wish, and crop it. Enlarge it to the size that you want for your completed artwork and make a print of the image either in black and white or in color.

"The only light that really exists [is] that in the artist's brain."
HENRI MATISSE

MAKING CROPPERS

You can make a pair of croppers out of a file folder. Using a ruler, draw a line 1" from the top and 1" from the right side of the folder. Then use an X-Acto knife to cut out an L-shaped piece (see photo at right). Repeat the process on the file folder's bottom left corner. You now have two L-shaped croppers.

Use a ruler and an X-Acto knife to cut out two L-shaped croppers.

STEP 3
TRACING THE IMAGE

Once you have decided on the image and focal area, the next step is to trace it onto tracing paper or vellum. But you will have to be careful. In portraits, when light falls on a subject's face, there are usually lighter areas on the cheekbones, eyelids, forehead, and chin. However, even if the light and dark areas blend together in the photograph, you have to decide where the light shape ends and the dark shape begins.

Be cautious about tracing every single line and shadow in the subject's face. When these lines are stitched in your finished artwork, they may prematurely *age* the face. If your subject is a child, a young person, or a woman, be especially judicious about which lines to include in your drawing. In "Nostalgic Portrait" I decided to make use of the dramatic shadows in Ida's and Anthony's faces, but in creating a "softer" portrait, you should carefully choose which lines to include and which to delete. For example, compare the two drawings above right. Especially on a child's face, the extra lines make a big difference.

STEP 4
DRAWING THE SHAPES

Once your drawing is complete, go over all the pencil lines with a black Pentel marker. Or if you like, darken the lines by using a copier machine set on a dark setting and copying your drawing onto an 8½"-x-11" piece of acetate. (If necessary, use additional pieces of acetate and tape them together.)

Next, make two 50 percent-reduction paper copies of the pattern. These small copies will be used to create your rough fabric paste-up in Step 2 on page 100.

"Everyone knows that even a single line may convey an emotion."
PIET MONDRIAN

With portraits of children, it's always best to delete excess facial lines.

As you can see, you will age your subject if you include every line on the child's face (see Step 3).

This is "P.J., Cute As a Button," 18" x 17" (2000). P.J. Casey. Private Collection.

Completing Your Artwork

STEP 1

Now that your pattern is completed, choose a variety of fabrics for each of the shapes in your pattern. Even though the Vacirca wedding photograph was in black and white, I chose fabrics in sepia tones—shades of browns and beiges—to create an old-fashioned effect (see photo above right). But if it appeals to you, choose an entirely different color scheme for your portrait: psychedelic colors from the '60s (see photo below left as an example), disco fabrics from the '80s, or even contemporary colors that are currently in fashion.

These fabric pieces show a range of browns and beiges that are possibilities for a sepia-toned portrait.

STEP 2

Make your final fabric choices by juxtaposing fabrics on top of your pattern. To make your portrait even more personal, consider using fabrics that are similar to, or actually from, the clothing that your subjects wore (see photo below right). For instance, you could use lace left over from your mother's wedding dress, satin from one of your father's ties, etc. Or use fabrics that remind you of the time period of your subjects. There are many fabrics available today that evoke earlier decades.

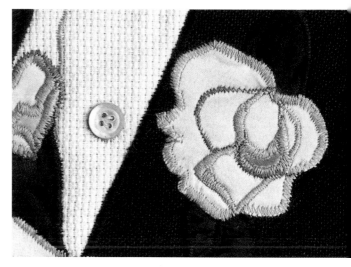

I stitched an actual button onto Anthony Vacirca's shirt and sewed a small piece of fabric underneath it that created a "shadow" effect (see Step 2).

After you have made your final choices, create a rough fabric paste-up. (If you need help in creating a rough fabric paste-up, see page 42 for instructions.)

This is a portrait, "LSD", that I created to show the effects of experimenting with drugs (see Step 1). 22" x 18" (1972)

STEP 3

Cut out generous pieces of your chosen fabrics. Set your iron on "cotton" and press them, using spray starch and ironing the fabric on the back. Next, iron paper-backed fusible webbing onto the backs of your fabric pieces, taking care not to iron the fusible webbing onto your ironing board surface.

STEP 4

Using the light box, trace the pattern shapes onto the backs of your fabric pieces.

STEP 5

Cut out the backing fabric. Iron it using spray starch.

STEP 6

Consider padding either the shapes or the entire artwork. If you do, cut out batting or felt padding according to the instructions on selective padding in Chapter 6, beginning on page 77, or on overall padding in Chapter 7, beginning on page 85.

STEP 7

Cut out the fabric shapes and position them *wrong side up* on the sticky board. (If you need help to make a sticky board, see page 47 for instructions.)

STEP 8

Remove the paper backing of the fusible webbing from the backs of the cut shapes. Lightly spray them with spray adhesive.

STEP 9

Tape the pattern *right side up* on the light box. Tape down the backing fabric. Then position the shapes on the backing fabric.

STEP 10

Fuse the shapes down by ironing them in place.

STEP 11

Machine-sew the shapes with a zigzag stitch.

STEP 12

Add embellishments, decorative stitching, or whatever you like. Complete the artwork by making it into a hanging or pillow. You could also staple it onto canvas stretchers, wood, or foam core, and frame it.

To complete "Nostalgic Portrait" I added a fabric back (*right side to right side*) and stitched it on three sides. Then I turned it right side out, inserted foam core, and closed the open side with hand-stitching. The portrait was later mounted on a double ply mat board and framed (see photo below right).

HINT
When you choose thread colors for the lines in the subjects' faces, pick colors that are just *slightly* darker than the color of the face itself. Experiment with different thread colors on a scrap piece of the face fabrics to decide which thread colors work best.

Here is Ida and Anthony Vacirca's wedding photograph and the framed stitched artwork.

People

People. I really enjoy looking at them, all kinds: anonymous faces in stacks of old photographs at flea markets or black-and-white photos of "everyday" people in the daily newspapers. But, most of all, I'm intrigued by their variety and inherent beauty. I've always enjoyed the challenge of capturing a likeness. Given the opportunity, I include friends and family in my artwork.

Mission Sunday
43" x 41" (1994)
Detail from "A Time for Hope" stitched artwork commissioned for the lobby of Bishop Francis J. Mugavero Center for Geriatric Care—Saint Vincent Catholic Medical Centers of New York. Architect: Joseph Marino. Year Created: 1994. Permission Granted: 2005.

My Family Quilt
5" x 6" (2001)
Commissioned by Harcourt, Inc.
Reproduced by permission of the publisher.

Girl with Ornament
11" x 9" (1984)
Originally published in *Woman's Day* Magazine

Flagler Portrait
17" x 14" (1986)
© 1986 *Palm Beach Life* Magazine

Old Fashioned Woman
24" x 18" (1974)

The First Noel
16¼" x 13¼" (1983)
Commissioned by Harcourt, Brace,
Jovanovich, Inc. for *The Christmas
Carol Sampler*

Marilyn Monroe
30" x 25" (1974)
TM Marilyn Monroe, LLC
by CMG Worldwide, Inc. /
www.MarilynMonroe.com

*"There is nothing more interesting
than people. One paints and one
draws to learn to see people,
to see oneself."*
PABLO PICASSO

Hugs and Kisses
14" x 12¼" (1991)
Commissioned by Macmillan for
A Quilt Full of Memories by Joanne Ryder.
Courtesy of The McGraw-Hill Companies, Inc.

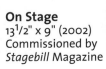

On Stage
13½" x 9" (2002)
Commissioned by
Stagebill Magazine

CHAPTER 9

Embellishing Your Fabric Artwork

I love holidays: dressing up on New Year's Eve, sparklers and fireworks on the Fourth of July, trick-or-treaters at Halloween, turkey on Thanksgiving. And then there's Christmas, my favorite by far.

When I was a child, decorating the Christmas tree was always a special treat, and my husband and I have carried on this tradition with our own family. This "Holiday Tree" image originally appeared on the cover of *Woman's Day Christmas Crafts* Magazine and was inspired by a catalog cover that I had created for Lord & Taylor department stores. That image is shown on page 107 and has more than three hundred ornaments! Luckily this "Holiday Tree" project is simpler, and I hope it will be a colorful decoration for your home or make a festive gift. In this chapter you will create "Holiday Tree," with its quilted background, appliquéd tree, window frame, and snowflakes. Decorate the tree with embellishments: beads, bits of jewelry, buttons, and charms.

Holiday Tree (Detail)
14" x 12" (2001)
Commissioned by Husqvarna Viking Sewing Machines
for *Woman's Day Christmas Crafts* Magazine

Making the Quilted Background

MATERIALS NEEDED

In addition to the materials in the General Materials Needed lists on pages 30 and 40, you will need the following:

18" metal ruler

red satin fabric, 18" x 16"

fabric, approximately 8" x 8" of each:

> **green textured fabric** (for the tree)
>
> **light blue satin fabric** (for the sky)
>
> **tan cotton fabric** (for the window frame)
>
> **white textured fabric** (for the snowdrifts)
>
> **white satin fabric** (for the snowflakes)
>
> **brown fabric** (for the tree trunk)

white cotton duck fabric, 18" x 16"

lightweight white batiste fabric, 10" x 10"

lightweight cotton padding, 16" x 16" (felt or cotton batting)

X-Acto knife

canvas stretchers (to make a 14"-x-12" frame)

foam core, 14" x 12" (*optional*)

white artist's tape, 1" wide (low tack tape with no residue)

decorations for the tree: charms, sequins, beads, bits of jewelry, etc.

brass metal star, 3/4" diameter

hair wire (thin wire available at hardware or craft stores)

I made my final fabric choices for "Holiday Tree" from these possibilities (see Step 1).

Follow the instructions below to complete the "Holiday Tree" artwork. To help simplify the information, I've divided them into two parts: "Making the Quilted Background" and "Making the Window/Tree Area." If you need more detailed information on creating stitched artwork from a pattern, refer back to Steps 1 to 11 on pages 40 to 49.

To make "Holiday Tree," enlarge the "Holiday Tree" pattern that appears on page 125 to the size that suits you and copy it onto tracing paper, vellum, or acetate. I have made my version 14" x 12", and this size works with the dimensions of the fabrics listed in the Materials Needed list. I've also listed suggested colors and fabrics, but feel free to make the fabric and color choices that appeal to you.

STEP 1

Choose a variety of fabrics for the quilted background (see photo above).

STEP 2

Make your final fabric choice for the quilted background by juxtaposing the different red fabrics on top of the pattern in relation to the fabrics of the window/tree area (see "Making the Window/Tree Area," Step 2 on page 108.)

STEP 3

Cut out a 18"-x-16" piece of the fabric chosen for the red quilted background. Set your iron on "cotton" and press them, using spray starch and ironing the fabric on the back.

STEP 4

Enlarge the pattern on page 126 that shows the layout of the white artist's tape on the red fabric. Place your pattern on the light box *right side up* and tape it down. Attach the red fabric *right side up* on top of the pattern using several small pieces of tape. Attach long strips of white artist's tape all around at the outer edges of the red fabric and also 1/2" inside the edges of the window/tree area. Make certain that the pieces of tape overlap each other at the corners. (This tape will help keep the fabric from shifting as you stitch the diamond pattern onto the red fabric in Step 7.)

Following the "Holiday Tree" pattern, trace the diamond-quilting pattern onto the front surface of the red fabric using the metal ruler and a red Pigma Micron or LePlume marker (pens that make thin lines, just dark enough for you to see them). Extend the lines $^1/2"$ inside the window/tree area in the center.

STEP 5

Cut out a 18"-x-16" piece of the white cotton duck backing fabric. Set your iron on "cotton" and press the fabric, using spray starch. Set it aside for use in Step 6.

STEP 6

Enlarge the "Holiday Tree" Padding pattern that appears on page 126. Trace it onto the padding and cut out the shape. Lightly spray adhesive on the backs of the padding and the red fabric.

Then make a "sandwich" of the red fabric, padding, and backing fabric. (For more information on overall padding and "sandwiches," see pages 48 and 88.) (*Optional:* Also baste the three layers together by hand.)

STEP 7

To create the quilted-diamond effect on the red fabric, machine-sew a running stitch with red thread on the red lines that you traced in Step 4. Start each line just inside the white tape on the outer edges and sew up to the tape in the center area.

After completing the stitching, remove the white tape from the quilted fabric. Set the quilted fabric aside for use in Step 9 of the window/tree area instructions.

HINT
Sew from north to south and then from east to west. (If you are not consistent, the quilted effect will be irregular.)

This is "Quilted Christmas Tree (Lord & Taylor)," 18" x 15" (1998), with more than three hundred ornaments on it.
Christmas 1998 Cover Design

Making the Window/Tree Area

STEP 1

Choose a variety of fabrics for each of the shapes in the window/tree area. The colors and fabrics are listed in the Materials Needed list on page 106, but feel free to make whatever choices appeal to you.

STEP 2

Make your final fabric choices by juxta-posing fabrics on top of the "Holiday Tree" pattern in relation to the red fabric of the quilted background. Then create a rough fabric paste-up. (If you need help in creating a rough fabric paste-up, see page 42 for instructions.)

STEP 3

Based on your rough fabric paste-up, cut out generous pieces of your fabrics. Set your iron on "cotton" and press them, using spray starch and ironing the fabric on the back. Next, iron paper-backed fusible webbing onto the backs of your fabric pieces, taking care not to iron the fusible webbing onto your ironing board surface.

STEP 4

Tape the pattern to the light box *wrong side up* and trace the shapes onto the backs of the green, white, light blue, brown, and tan fabrics. Remember to allow for a $1/8$" underlap where the shapes are next to each other in the drawing (for example, where the green tree shape overlaps the tree trunk, allow $1/8$" extra at the top of the trunk shape).

    Trace the light blue sky fabric as one $5^3/4$" x $5^3/4$" shape.

STEP 5

Cut out a 10"-x-10" square of white lightweight batiste fabric to be used to back the window/tree area. Set your iron on "cotton" and press the fabric, using spray starch.

STEP 6

Using the "Holiday Tree" pattern from page 125, cut out a padding shape that is $1/8$" smaller all around than the shape of the tree. Set this aside for use in Step 9. (For more information on selective padding, see Chapter 6, beginning on page 77; for more information on overall padding, see Chapter 7, beginning on page 85.)

Your choice of ornaments and decorations will personalize your "Holiday Tree."

STEP 7

Cut out all the fabric shapes and position them on the sticky board *wrong side up.* (If you need help to make a sticky board, see page 47 for instructions.)

(*Optional*) To cut out the snowflakes, use an X-Acto knife and/or sharp scissors. If this is too difficult, try this: Draw the lines for the snowflakes' outside edges and also for the inside shapes, but don't cut out the inside shapes. Later you can paint those shapes with light blue paint and/or machine-sew a zigzag stitch over them using a light blue thread that matches the light blue fabric of the sky (see photo at right). If neither alternative works for you and you find that snowflakes are just too difficult, then eliminate them.

STEP 8

Remove the paper backing of the fusible webbing from the backs of the cut shapes. Lightly spray the backs of the shapes with spray adhesive.

STEP 9

With the "Holiday Tree" pattern taped *right side up* on the light box, position the 10"-x-10" backing fabric shapes on top of the pattern. Then, using tweezers, position the shapes on top of it in this order: light blue sky, snowdrifts, snowflakes, window frame, tree trunk, padding for the tree shape, and finally green tree fabric.

STEP 10

Set your iron on "cotton." Cover the shapes with a pressing cloth. Fuse the shapes down by ironing them in place.

The appliquéd snowflakes are optional, but they add a lot of charm to "Holiday Tree" (see Step 7).

STEP 11

Machine-sew the shapes down with a zigzag stitch, using thread that matches the color of each fabric. However, do not stitch the outside edges of the window frame, the top 1" of the tree, or the bottom of the tree trunk. (These areas will be stitched later.) Trim off the excess backing fabric just to the edge of the window frame.

Lightly spray adhesive onto the back of the window/tree area. Position it in the center of the red quilted background. Using thread that matches the color of each fabric, zigzag-stitch the outside edges of the window frame, the top 1" of the tree, and the bottom edge of the tree trunk.

STEP 12

Staple the stitched artwork onto canvas stretchers or a piece of $1/2$" foam core.

"Art is a language of symbols."
PABLO PICASSO

Decorating "Holiday Tree"

This is the fun part—now you get to decorate your tree. Gather beads, brass charms, buttons, bits of jewelry, etc. and enjoy yourself (see photo at top left for suggestions).

Cut out a tree shape from a scrap piece of the green fabric that you used for "Holiday Tree." Position your decorations on the tree fabric. Move the ornaments and garlands around on top of the green fabric. When you are happy with the layout, carefully remove each decoration, one by one, and attach it to the stitched tree in the position that you've chosen for it. Use white glue or stitching to attach each decoration to the tree. End with the gold star.

ATTACHING THE ORNAMENTS TO THE TREE

For garlands, string beads onto thin hair wire to make graceful curves. Then glue or stitch them in position (see photo below at top right).

Before gluing down each decoration, create a depression—a "dimple" effect—in the tree fabric with a straight pin (or by hand-sewing a few small stitches) so that your decorations will appear to be sunk into the tree (see photo below at bottom left). The decorations will cover the pin or the stitches (see photo below at bottom right.)

There are so many decorations you can add to your tree.

By stringing the beads on wire rather than on thread, the bead garlands will maintain their curved shapes when you attach them to the tree.

If you have mounted your "Holiday Tree" onto foam core, use a pin to create a "dimple" before gluing down each decoration. If you have mounted it onto canvas stretchers, use hand-stitching to make the "dimple."

Glue a bead or other decoration in place on top of the "dimple."

Holidays

This gallery includes many of my favorite images. The time between holidays was the way I measured my childhood. I hope this artwork will inspire you to create holiday images of your own.

Santa Claus (with Toy)
13" x 10" (1984)
Originally published in *Woman's Day* Magazine

O Christmas Tree
20" x 16" (1983)
Commissioned by Harcourt, Brace, Jovanovich, Inc.
for *The Christmas Carol Sampler*

Family in Blue Landscape
14 1/2" x 14 1/4"
Commissioned by Amana Corporation for
Daimaru Department Store

Holiday Lane
28" x 22" (1987)
Commissioned by Macy's for a poster

Valentine's Day: Katie
14" x 19" (1981)
Commissioned by Avon Products, Inc. for 1986 Centennial
Avon calendar. Collection of Frank X. Cusack

St. Patrick's Day: Kites Flying
17" x 15" (1985)
Commissioned by Avon Products, Inc. for 1986
Centennial Avon calendar. Collection of Ron and
Otti Breland.

May Day
16" x 15" (1985)
Commissioned by Avon Products, Inc. for 1986
Centennial Avon calendar

*"A pictorial work . . . is constructed bit by bit,
just like a house."*
PAUL KLEE

Statue of Liberty
17" x 16" (1985)
Commissioned by Avon Products, Inc. for 1986
Centennial Avon calendar

Mom with Turkey
14" x 11" (1984)
Originally published in *Woman's Day* Magazine

Children at the Beach
16" x 15" (1985)
Commissioned by Avon Products, Inc. for 1986
Centennial Avon calendar

Witch
24" x 18" (1974)

Easter Morning
9¹/₂" x 8¹/₂" (1997)
Commissioned by Bookspan
(formerly Doubleday Direct, Inc.)

Patterns

"DOWN ON THE FARM"
(Instructions begin on page 39.)

"Down on the Farm"

"FLORAL BORDER"

(Instructions begin on page 58.)

"Floral Border" Pillow

"Floral Border" Greeting Card
(photograph is inserted in the oval center)

Cardboard A

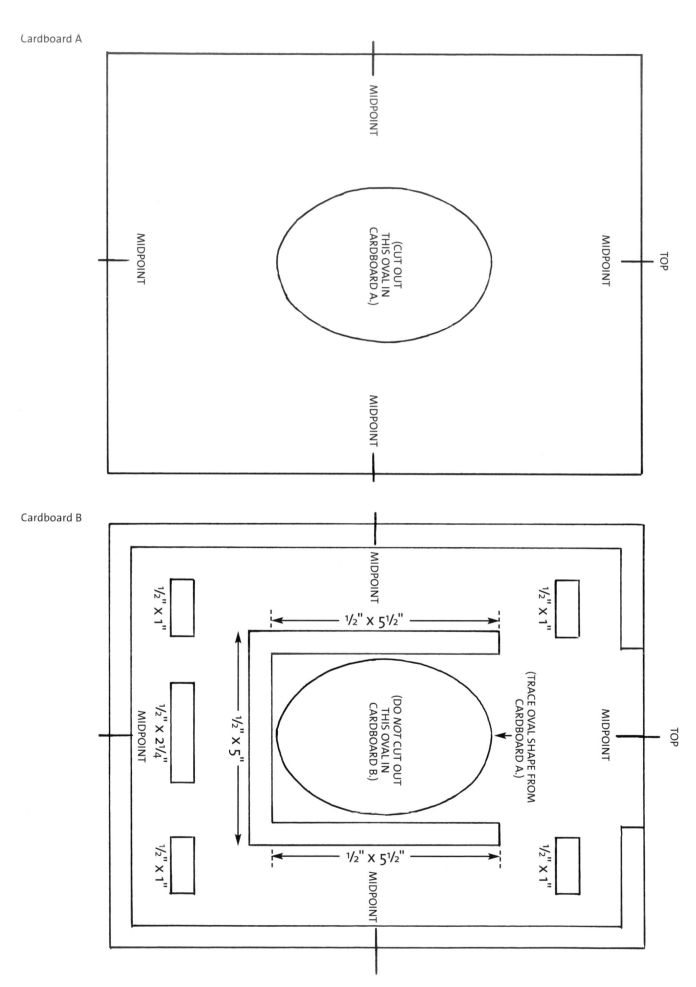

MIDPOINT

MIDPOINT

MIDPOINT

TOP

(CUT OUT
THIS OVAL IN
CARDBOARD A.)

MIDPOINT

Cardboard B

MIDPOINT

MIDPOINT

TOP

½" x 1"

½" x 1"

½" x 5½"

½" x 2¼"

½" x 5"

(DO *NOT* CUT OUT
THIS OVAL IN
CARDBOARD B.)

(TRACE OVAL SHAPE FROM
CARDBOARD A.)

MIDPOINT

½" x 1"

½" x 1"

½" x 5½"

MIDPOINT

"Floral Border" Picture Frame

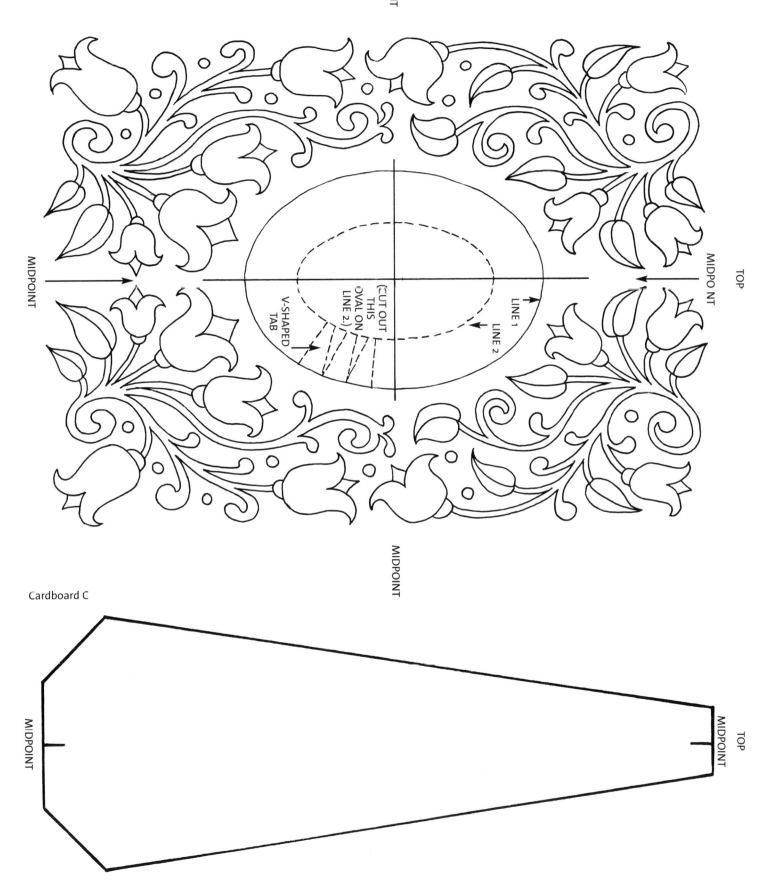

MIDPOINT

MIDPOINT

MIDPOINT

MIDPOINT

TOP

LINE 1

LINE 2

(CUT OUT
THIS
OVAL ON
LINE 2.)

V-SHAPED
TAB

Cardboard C

MIDPOINT

TOP
MIDPOINT

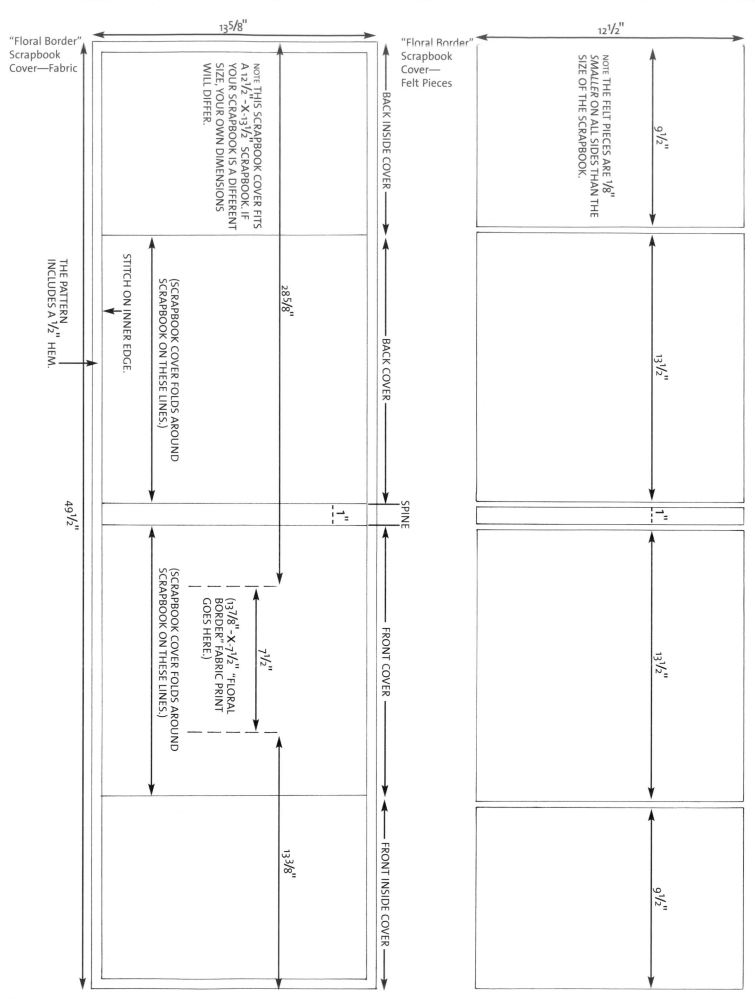

"Floral Border" Scrapbook Cover—Fabric

13⅝"

"Floral Border" Scrapbook Cover—Felt Pieces

12½"

NOTE THIS SCRAPBOOK COVER FITS A 12½"-X-13½" SCRAPBOOK. IF YOUR SCRAPBOOK IS A DIFFERENT SIZE, YOUR OWN DIMENSIONS WILL DIFFER.

BACK INSIDE COVER

NOTE THE FELT PIECES ARE ⅛" SMALLER ON ALL SIDES THAN THE SIZE OF THE SCRAPBOOK.

9½"

STITCH ON INNER EDGE.

(SCRAPBOOK COVER FOLDS AROUND SCRAPBOOK ON THESE LINES.)

28⅝"

BACK COVER

13½"

THE PATTERN INCLUDES A ½" HEM.

49½"

1"

SPINE

1"

(13⅞"-X-7½" "FLORAL BORDER" FABRIC PRINT GOES HERE.)

7½"

FRONT COVER

13½"

(SCRAPBOOK COVER FOLDS AROUND SCRAPBOOK ON THESE LINES.)

13⅜"

FRONT INSIDE COVER

9½"

"Welcome Home" Banner

(Instructions begin on page 68.)

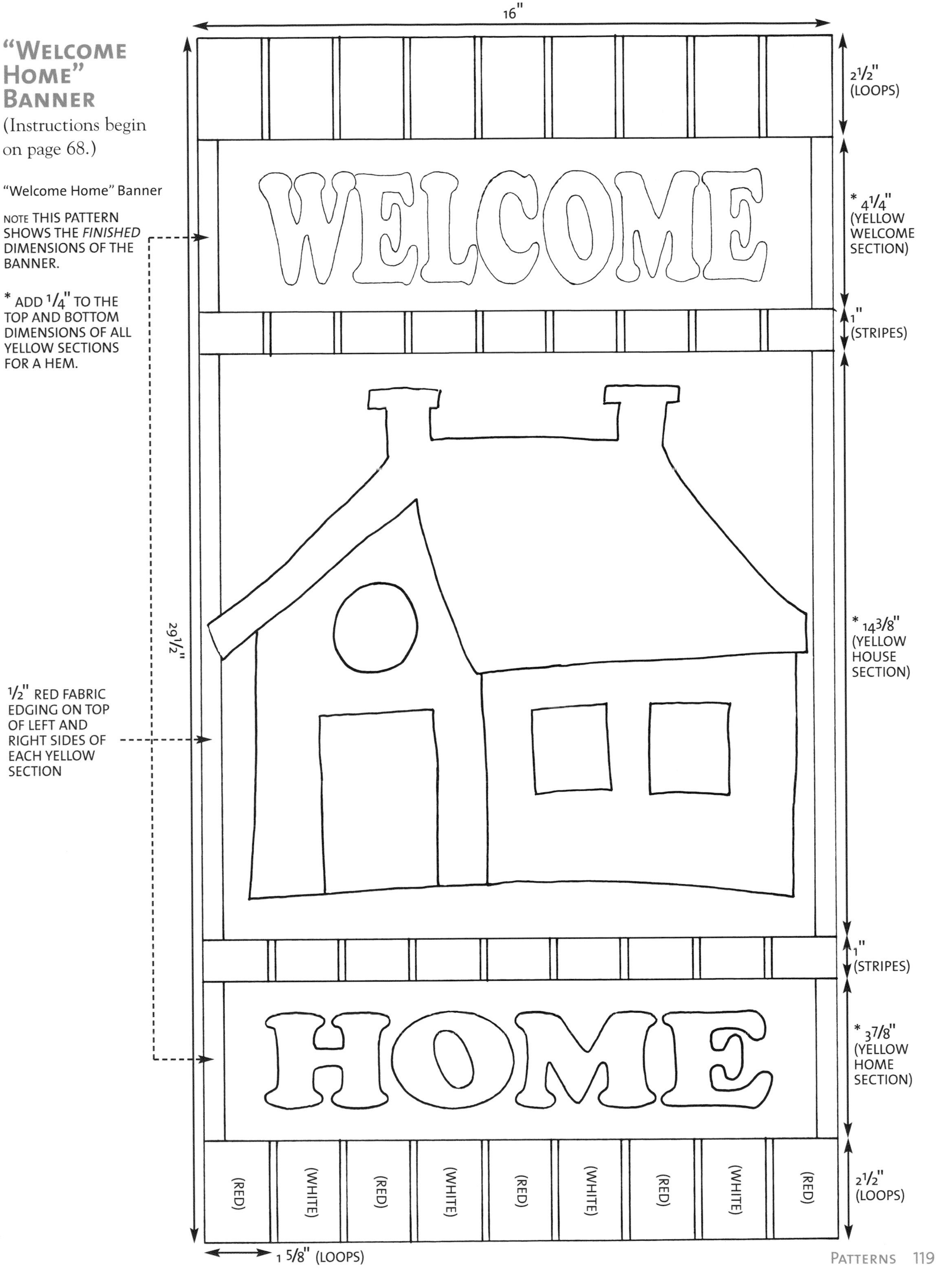

"Welcome Home" Banner

NOTE THIS PATTERN SHOWS THE *FINISHED* DIMENSIONS OF THE BANNER.

* ADD 1/4" TO THE TOP AND BOTTOM DIMENSIONS OF ALL YELLOW SECTIONS FOR A HEM.

1/2" RED FABRIC EDGING ON TOP OF LEFT AND RIGHT SIDES OF EACH YELLOW SECTION

16"

2 1/2" (LOOPS)

* 4 1/4" (YELLOW WELCOME SECTION)

1" (STRIPES)

29 1/2"

* 14 3/8" (YELLOW HOUSE SECTION)

1" (STRIPES)

* 3 7/8" (YELLOW HOME SECTION)

2 1/2" (LOOPS)

(RED) (WHITE) (RED) (WHITE) (RED) (WHITE) (RED) (WHITE) (RED)

1 5/8" (LOOPS)

WELCOME

HOME

ABCDEFGH
IJKLMNOPQ
RSTUVWX
YZ [&;!?]

TOP

ABCDEFGHIJK
LMNOPQRSTUV
WXYZ (&;!?)

Personalized Name Section

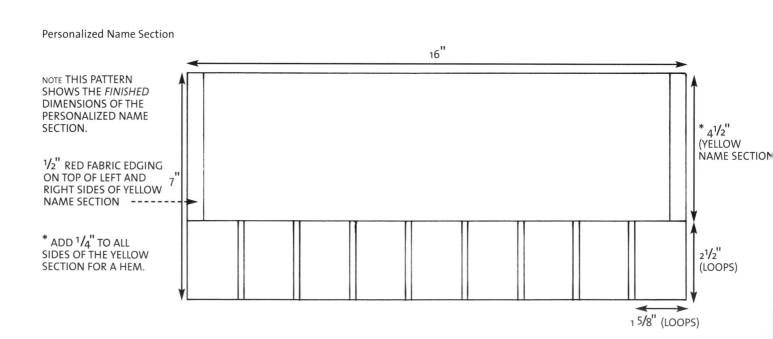

NOTE THIS PATTERN SHOWS THE *FINISHED* DIMENSIONS OF THE PERSONALIZED NAME SECTION.

1/2" RED FABRIC EDGING ON TOP OF LEFT AND RIGHT SIDES OF YELLOW NAME SECTION

* ADD 1/4" TO ALL SIDES OF THE YELLOW SECTION FOR A HEM.

16"

* 4 1/2" (YELLOW NAME SECTION)

7"

2 1/2" (LOOPS)

1 5/8" (LOOPS)

"VASE OF FLOWERS"

(Instructions begin on page 78.)

"Vase of Flowers"

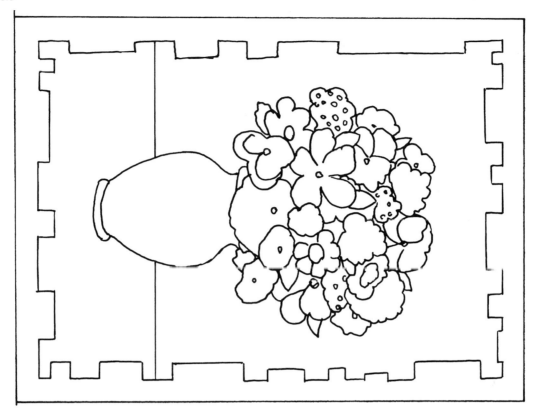

"Vase of Flowers" Stem Structure

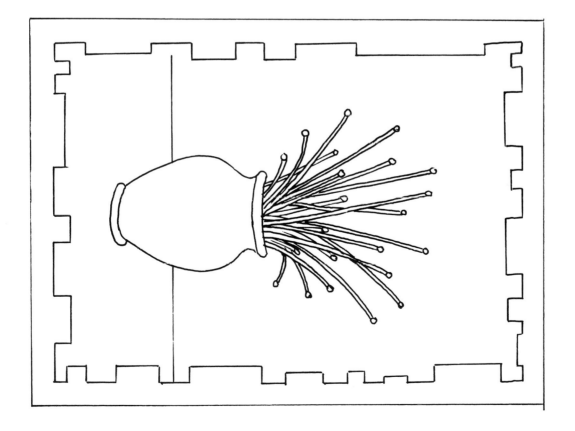

"Family Tree" Hanging
(Instructions begin on page 86.)

"Family Tree"
(with no labels)

"Family Tree"
(with seven
labels)

"Family Tree" (with eight labels)

"Family Tree"
(with nine
labels)

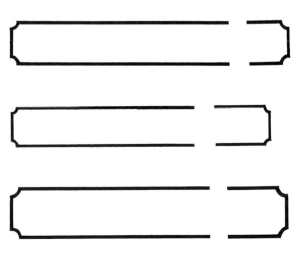

Label Border

"NOSTALGIC PORTRAIT"

(Instructions begin on page 96.)

"Nostalgic
Portrait"

"HOLIDAY TREE"
(Instructions begin on page 106.)

"Holiday Tree" patterns commissioned by
Husqvarna Viking Sewing Machines for *Woman's
Day Christmas Crafts* Magazine

"Holiday Tree"

Layout of the white artist's tape on red fabric of "Holiday Tree"

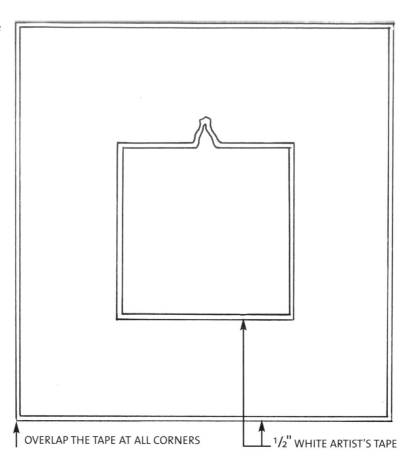

↑ OVERLAP THE TAPE AT ALL CORNERS   ½" WHITE ARTIST'S TAPE

Padding pattern for red quilted fabric area of "Holiday Tree"

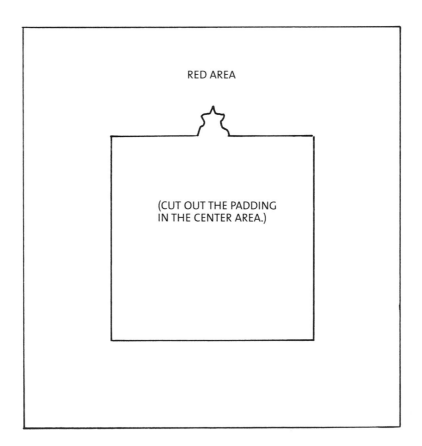

RED AREA

(CUT OUT THE PADDING IN THE CENTER AREA.)

Resources

Selected Materials and Equipment

Most of the supplies for the projects in *Picture Your World in Appliqué* are available at local fabric stores and art stores. Listed below are the manufacturers of some of the materials used in this book. Most of these companies sell their products exclusively to art supply, crafts, and fabric retailers, which are a consumer's most dependable sources for appliqué and quilting supplies. Your local retailers can advise you on purchases, and if you need something they don't have in stock, they will usually order it for you. If you can't find a store in your area that carries a particular item or will accept a request for an order, or if you need special assistance, a manufacturer will direct you to the retailer nearest you that carries its products and will try to answer any technical questions you might have.

Artograph, Inc.
Vicksburg Lane North
Plymouth, MN 55447
(888) 975-9555;
(763) 553-1112, 2838
www.artograph.com
Artograph

Clover Needlecraft Inc.
13438 Alondra Boulevard
Cerritos, CA 90703
(800) 233-1703; (562) 282-0200
www.clover-usa.com
paper-backed fusible webbing

Coats & Clark
Consumer Services
P.O. Box 12229
Greenville, SC 29612-0229
(800) 648-1479
www.coatsandclark.com
threads

Elmers Products Inc.
2020 West Front Street
Statesville, NC 28687
(800) 873-4868
www.forframersonly.com
tacking iron

Golden Threads
2 South 373 Seneca Drive
Wheaton, IL 60187
(888) 477-7718
www.goldenthreads.com
tear-away paper

June Tailor Inc.
P.O. Box 208
2861 Highway 175
Richfield, WI 53076
(800) 844-5400; (262) 644-5288
www.junetailor.com
paper-backed fabric

Milliken & Co.
920 Milliken Road
Spartanburg, SC 29303
(864) 503-2020
www.milliken.com
paper-backed fabric

Neschen USA, L.L.C.
9800 West York
Wichita, KS 67215
(877) 637-2436; (316) 522-9438
www.neschenusa.com/library/
adhesives.html
Gudy mounting adhesives

Piedmont Plastics, Inc.
5010 West W.T. Harris Boulevard
P.O. Box 26006
Charlotte, NC 28269
(800) 277-7898; (704) 597-8200
Gudy mounting adhesives

Therm O Web
770 Glenn Avenue
Wheeling, IL 60090
(847) 520-5200
www.thermoweb.com
paper-backed fusible webbing

3M Corporate Headquarters
3M Center
St. Paul, MN 55144-1000
(888) 364-3577
www.3m.com/us/mfg_industrial/
adhesives/framing/html/
spraymount.jhtml
3M Spray Mount Artist's Adhesive

Troy Corporation
2701 North Normandy Avenue
Chicago, IL 60707
(800) 888-2400
www.troy-corp.com
iron-on polyester twill

Selected Publications

American Quilter Magazine
P.O. Box 3290
Paducah, KY 42002-3290
(502) 898-7903
www.americanquilter.com

Fiberarts Magazine
201 East Fourth Street
Loveland, CO 80537
(800) 272-2193
www.fiberartsmagazine.com

Needlearts Magazine
335 West Broadway, Suite 100
Louisville, KY 40402-2105
(502) 589-6956
www.egausa.org

The Professional Quilter
22412 Rolling Hill Lane
Laytonsville, MD 20882
www.professionalquilter.com

Quilters Newsletter Magazine
741 Corporate Circle, Suite A
Golden, CO 80401-5644
(800) 477-6089
www.qnm.com

Surface Design Journal
P.O. Box 360
Sebastopol, CA 95473-0360
(707) 829-3110
www.surfacedesign.org

Threads Magazine
The Taunton Press
63 Main Street, Box 5506
Newtown, CT 06470-5506
(800) 309-9262; (203) 304-3523
www.threadsmagazine.com

Selected Organizations

American Craft Council
72 Spring Street, 6th floor
New York, NY 10012
(212) 274-0630
www.craftcouncil.org
national organization promoting crafts

American Quilter's Society
P.O. Box 3290
Paducah, KY 42002-3290
(502) 898-7903
www.americanquilter.com
national organization promoting quilting

The Embroiderers' Guild
of America, Inc.
335 West Broadway, Suite 100
Louisville, KY 40402-2105
(502) 589-6956
www.egausa.org
national organization promoting embroidery

Graphic Artist Guild
90 John Street, Suite 403
New York, NY 10038-3202
(212) 791-3400
www.gag.org
national organization promoting the interests of artists

Society of Children's Book Writers
and Illustrators
8271 Beverly Boulevard
Los Angeles, CA 90048
(323) 782-1010
www.scbwi.org
international organization of children's book writers and illustrators

Studio Art Quilt Associates
P.O. Box 572
Storrs, CT 06268-0572
(860) 487-4198
www.saqa.com
international organization of quilt artists

Surface Design Association
P.O. Box 360
Sebastopol, CA 95473-0360
(707) 829-3110
www.surfacedesign.org
international organization promoting textiles

Textile Society of America
P.O. Box 70
Earleville, MD 21919
(410) 275-2329
www.textilesociety.org
international organization promoting textiles

Textile Study Group of New York
P.O. Box 721
New York, NY 10014
www.tsgny.org
international organization promoting fiber artwork

Suggested Reading

Stitched Artwork Techniques

Anderson, Charlotte Warr. *Focus on Features*. Lafayette, Calif.: C&T Publishing, 1998.

Avery, Virginia. *The Big Book of Applique for Quilts (and Banners, Clothes, Hangings, Gifts, & More)*. New York: Charles Scribner's Sons, 1978.

Carlson, Susan E. *Free-Style Quilts: A "No Rules" Approach*. Lafayette, Calif.: C&T Publishing, 2000.

Davenport, Allen Bragdon. *The Family Creative Workshop*, vol. 1.

New York: Plenary Publications, 1974.

Fanning, Robbie, and Tony Fanning. *The Complete Book of Machine Embroidery*. Radnor, Penn.: Chilton Book Company, 1986.

Gordon, Maggie McCormick. *Pictorial Quilting*. New York: Watson-Guptill Publications, 2000.

Greco, Nick, and Kathleen Ziegler. *Fabric Sculpture: The Step-by-Step Guide and Showcase*. Rockport, Mass.: Rockport Publisher, 1995.

Hackett, Mary L. *A Bridge to Landscape Quilts*. Paducah, Ky.: American Quilter's Society, 2004.

Hall, Carolyn. *The Sewing Machine Craft Book*. New York: Van Nostrand Reinhold Company, 1980.

Hall, Carolyn Vosburg. *Pictorial Quilts: Stitch an Art Quilt by Hand or Machine*. Radnor, Penn.: Chilton Book Company, 1993.

Nadelstern, Paula. *Kaleidoscopes & Quilts*. Lafayette, Calif.: C&T Publishing, Inc., 1996.

Newman, Thelma R., Lee Scott Newman, and Jay Hartley Newman. *Sewing Machine Embroidery and Stitchery: Techniques, Inspiration, and Projects for Embroidery, Appliqué, Quilting, Patchwork, and Trapunto*. New York: Crown Publishers, Inc., 1980.

Rixford, Ellen. *3-Dimensional Illustration*. New York: Watson-Guptill Publications, 1993.

Sienkiewicz, Elly. *Appliqué 12 Easy Ways!* Lafayette, Calif.: C&T Publishing, Inc., 1991.

Inspiration

Batchelder, Ann, and Nancy Orban. *Fiberarts Design Books #7*. Asheville, N.C.: Lark Books, 2004.

Brown, Clint. *Artist to Artist: Inspiration & Advice from Artists Past & Present*. Corvallis, Oreg.: Jackson Creek Press, 1998.

Crow, Nancy. *Nancy Crow: Quilts and Influences*. Paducah, Ky.: American Quilter's Society, 1990.

Harris, Ann Sutherland, and Linda Nochlin. *Women Artists: 1550-1950*. New York: Alfred A. Knopf, 1976.

James, Michael. *Art & Inspirations*. Lafayette, Calif.: C&T Publishing, Inc., 1998.

Lavitt, Wendy. *Contemporary Pictorial Quilts*. Layton, Utah: Gibbs-Smith Publisher, 1993.

MacKay, William. *Envisioning Art: A Collection of Quotations by Artists*. New York: Barnes & Noble, Inc., 2003.

Robinson, Charlotte. *The Artist & The Quilt*. New York: Alfred A. Knopf, Inc., 1983.

Rosenberg, Judith Pierce. *Question of Balance: Artists and Writers on Motherhood*. Watsonville, Calif.: Papier-Mache Press, 1995.

Scherer, Deidre. *Work in Fabric & Thread*. Lafayette, Calif.: C&T Publishing, Inc., 1998.

Shaw, Robert. *The Art Quilt*. New York: Hugh, Lauter Levin Associates, 1997.

Smith, Barbara Lee. *Celebrating the Stitch*. Newtown, Conn.: The Taunton Press, 1991.

Tharp, Twyla. *The Creative Habit: Learn It and Use It for Life*. New York: Simon & Schuster, 2003.

Business and Reference

Association of Theatrical Artist and Craftspeople. *The Entertainment Sourcebook 2002 Edition (An Insider's Guide on Where to Find Everything)*. New York: Association of Theatrical Artist and Craftspeople, 2002.

Crawford, Tad. *Business and Legal Forms for Graphic Designers*, 3d ed. New York: Allworth Press, 2003.

————. *Legal Guide for the Visual Artist*, 4th ed. New York: Allworth Press, Inc., 2001.

Fleishman, Michael. *Starting Your Career as a Freelance Illustrator or Graphic Designer*. New York: Allworth Press, 2003.

Graphic Artists Guild Handbook: Pricing and Ethical Guidelines, 10th ed. New York: Graphic Artists Guild, Inc., 2001.

Leland, Caryn R. *Licensing Art & Design*. New York: Allworth Press, Inc., 1995.

McCann, Michael. *Health Hazards Manual for Artists*, 5th ed. New York: The Lyons Press, 2003.

Rossol, Monona. *The Artist's Complete Health and Safety Guide*, 3d ed. New York: Allworth Press, 2001.

For more information and a list of books illustrated by Margaret Cusack, visit her Web site at www.MargaretCusack.com

Index